The Journal Of The Absurd

by
Jules Siegel
&
Bernard Garfinkel

Illustration
by
Diana Bryan

Workman Publishing
New York

Staff

Anita Brown; Malinda Thal; J. Nebraska Gifford;
Laura Fogelman; Dale Hoffer.

Published simultaneously in Canada by Saunders of Toronto, Inc.

Library of Congress Cataloging in Publication Data

Siegel, Jules.
    The journal of the absurd.

    1. Curiosities and wonders.   I. Garfinkel,
    Bernard,   joint author.   II. Title.
    AG243.S55   1980   031'.02   79-3887
    ISBN 0-89480-078-7 (pbk.)

Cover design: Jules Siegel

Workman Publishing
1 West 39 Street
New York, New York 10018

Manufactured in the United States of America
10 9 8 7 6 5 4 3 2 1

For Anita Brown
—Jules Siegel

For Peter and David Franck
—Bernard Garfinkel

Contents

Introduction

"Philosophy Is the Mind's Chewing Gum"

As any fool can plainly see, each and every one of the heartwarming dramas that litter these pages should have been a two-hour, prime-time TV special, produced, written, and directed by Siegel and Garfinkel.

That was the plan. But who has time to negotiate with network biggies who dangle thousands of mint-fresh greenbacks in front of you in an all-out, no-price-is-too-high battle to buy your material? Life is too short. Besides, we knew that the contents of this survival manual were too important, in these grave times, to feed them into television's slow-grinding mills. So here you are, out a few bucks, but the proud owner of this collection, forty thousand words of wisdom in an elegant paperback container.

What wisdom? You paid your money. Read the book and figure it out for yourself. But first, a word from our sponsor, Mr. Peter Workman, the modest genius who commands the far-flung resources of Workman Publishing. "Tell them why you called it *The Journal of the Absurd*," he barked, slapping his desk with a best-selling copy of B. Kliban's *Cat*. The dialogue that ensued, reprinted here in its entirety, may serve to shed some light on this startling and significant query.

GARFINKEL: Well, you have to admit it's an evocative and commercial title with excellent possibilities for promotion.

WORKMAN: That's no answer.

SIEGEL: Philosophy is the mind's chewing gum. There is a technique of classical logic called *reductio ad adsurdum*, in which you elaborate the possibilities of a situation until it becomes self-evidently absurd. We now find ourselves at exactly that point, as The Age of Reason exhausts itself into The Age of the Absurd. Thus this book.

WORKMAN: What?

SIEGEL: The *Oxford English Dictionary* defines absurd as, and I quote from memory, "Out of harmony with reason or propriety; incongruous, unreasonable, illogical. In modern use especially, plainly opposed to reason, and, *hence*, ridiculous, silly."

GARFINKEL: Right, the book is full of stuff that shouldn't happen but does—incidents and events that are illogical and unreasonable.

WORKMAN: Okay, that's a start. Put that in.

SIEGEL: *Jawohl*, Herr Ober.

GARFINKEL: Think of it in this way. A guy slips on a banana peel—

WORKMAN: That's funny, but it's not absurd.

GARFINKEL: Right. But say he slips, goes up in the air and does a double somersault before he comes down. That's absurd.

SIEGEL: Absolutely. Because it shouldn't happen.

GARFINKEL: That's it. But in this case, it only remains absurd if you don't know how and why it happened. Say the guy turns out to be an Olympic Gold winner in gymnastics. Once you know that, you don't think it's absurd anymore.

WORKMAN: So we can say that something is absurd if the result goes against our experience and knowledge, turns it upside down.

SIEGEL: You got it. That's why governments, scientists, engineers, and businessmen are most upset by the absurd. Their lives and triumphs are based on beliefs of authority and order and predictability. They don't like to get caught with their pants down, which is what happens when the absurd occurs.

GARFINKEL: Predictability is a big thing here. The result remains absurd even when you can explain it, if it's really startling, totally unexpected, not what happens ninety-nine times out of a hundred, totally unpredictable.

WORKMAN: But all these items aren't funny.

SIEGEL: Who said they had to be funny?

WORKMAN: You want the book to be a success, you ought to have funny items. People like to laugh—they don't like to read serious stuff.

GARFINKEL: Some of the serious stuff is so serious it makes you laugh.

WORKMAN: You, maybe. Not everyone.

SIEGEL: That may be because they're not concerned enough. We hope the book will make them concerned. But you have to understand that the absurd is more than just funny. It's more inclusive. Sometimes it makes you laugh. But it can also invoke strong feelings of panic, unreasoning dread—precisely because these serious things have happened, and they shouldn't have happened, it's absurd that they *have* happened.

WORKMAN: But what about the items that just don't seem absurd. For example, you've got one in which a pimp beats up a prostitute unmercifully, runs a steam iron down her back, and more. What's so absurd about that? That's just horrible.

GARFINKEL: You don't think that's absurd? You think that simply talking to another pimp, which was what she did that the pimp didn't like, is a serious enough crime for him to punish her that way? It's absurd precisely because it's so horrible.

SIEGEL: Of course, it's up to the reader to judge how absurd these items are. We consider every item in the book to be a reflection of one or another of the absurd aspects of life these days. The book is a Natural History of Our Times. There's a certain insanity operating. Those who don't see absurdity in some of the items may in that case have surrendered to this insanity. You could think of the items as a Rorschach test on absurdity.

GARFINKEL: I like that. It makes it a how-to book, as well as a funny and profound one. And one further thought: We've collected the research on which the items are based over the past few years from newspapers and other sources. Every single item is a report on the reality of our times. The tendency toward absurdity in this reality has been going on for a while, and no doubt it will continue. Call it the breakdown of an industrialized society. That's something that everyone can see in a different way, because we're all in the middle of it. Siegel and I didn't agree on every single item in the book. He liked some and I liked others. But we explained our feelings to each other. If the item stayed in, it was because we both finally agreed it *was* absurd. So the book is our reading on absurdity.

WORKMAN: Well, I'm glad you could work together that way.

SIEGEL: Yeah, it was a good partnership. Maybe we'll end up as well known as Simon & Garfunkel.

WORKMAN: Print it.

Siegel & Garfinkel

1
California

Does the absurd have a special habitat? Probably not. On the other hand, there's California, where a sizable portion of the population persists in viewing life as a B-movie. Hence the general passion for melodrama, sexual excess, cardboard personality, and tinsel-plated dialogue. For the absurd, in short.

History.

California was named after California, the heroine of a trashy 16th-century Spanish romantic novel that was the exact equivalent of a modern gothic and which was satirically parodied by Cervantes in *Don Quixote*.

Realism.

The state of California has announced that it will supply brassieres and female sex hormones to transsexual inmates at the Department of Corrections medical facility at Vacaville.

It Was Looking for the Bar.

A 45-pound octopus was found stuck to the floor of the ladies' room in the rooftop bar of San Francisco's Hyatt Regency Hotel. Six hotel employees using broom handles as levers finally pried the creature's powerful suction cups off the tiles and carted it off in a pail to the local aquarium.

There was no explanation of how the octopus ended up in the ladies' room.

How Happy?

Lois Faulkner, 68, was free on $100 bail in Ventura, California, for handing out free bags of marijuana to kids in the neighborhood. She did it, she said, because she wanted to make the children happy.

The Permissive Society.

In San Francisco, institutions, animals, and people perform wild, woolly, wonderful stunts, and the city fathers take it all in stride— as long as a permit has been granted. Every year, the city processes more than 2,000 permits, asking permission to do things, and as often as not, as witness the list below, permission is granted.

◉　A man was granted a permit to burn a piano on the beach and record the sounds as it was burning. He tied strings to each key of the piano and lit them one by one, recording the ensuing improvisation. Before starting, he had to obtain permits from a half dozen city agencies, including police, fire, and environmental pollution departments.

◉　Members of the Church of the Divine Light were given permission to burn all of their earthly possessions in a huge pyre overlooking the ocean. People tossed in fur coats and other expensive items.

◉　The Greenpeace Foundation sought a permit to parachute into the bay a massive, two-ton sculpture of a whale. It was turned down by the local agency, then overruled and granted a modified version of the permit by the mayor. The whale was later lowered by helicopter onto the Marina Green.

◉　A man was seized by police when he streaked naked through the band concourse in Golden Gate Park while the band was playing. Authorities later noted that he had a permit, but not a proper one.

◉   A man with an extremely loud pipe organ was granted permission by the city to play his instrument at the edge of the Oakland-San Francisco Bay Bridge as an arriving ship passed underneath. The ship probably heard the welcome, but so did harried motorists who later complained by the dozens to police about the noise.

◉   A city dog holds a special permit to climb trees in Golden Gate Park. TV's Bionic Dog is modeled after this dog.

◉   A man was granted a permit to create a huge "string sculpture" that looked more like a giant cat's cradle than anything else. It covered an entire meadow in Golden Gate Park.

◉   A group was granted a permit to build a pyramid at Embarcadero Plaza between several skyscrapers. The pyramid was used for meditation activities, as well as for popularizing the concept of "pyramid power."

◉   Numerous persons have sought permits for parades involving wild animals. Some have been denied. But the March of Dimes violated the San Francisco "permit spirit" by bringing a tiger and elephant into Golden Gate Park at the last minute of their fund-raising event. The Hari Krishnas have also marched elephants through Golden Gate Park.

Bernice Rogers has been San Francisco's head permit officer since 1970: "It's one of the most exciting jobs you could dream of," she says. "There's something happening every minute. I wouldn't want to have any other job."

Permission granted.

The Clean Society.

H ot tubs can be deadly, according to the Federal Consumer Product Safety Commission. Citing ten hot tub deaths in 1979, the agency urged pregnant women to avoid possible brain damage to the fetus in their early months, and warned all hot tub users not to drink heavily and to keep the water temperature below 104°.

"Soaking in a hot tub heated to 106° Fahrenheit can raise human body temperature to the point of heatstroke," the commission reported. "These conditions can be fatal even to fully healthy adults." Persons with heart disease, diabetes or blood pressure problems and those on various medications were also told to be careful.

Half of the deaths occurred in California.

Most Stubborn Flasher in San Francisco.

Larry Burnstin, 27, of Wendover, Nevada, was arrested in San Francisco after police spotted him at Mission and 18th streets standing in the nude chatting with pedestrians. Burnstin served 10 days and was released. Five minutes after a judge let him go, Burnstin was rearrested on the crowded second floor of the San Francisco Hall of Justice. Burnstin began by going through "warm-up exercises"—police jargon for unzipping zippers—but before the cops could reach him, he had taken off everything but his shirt.

As Burnstin was led away, a police officer reported that he had said: "I was just expressing my joy at being released."

Just Like a Man to Be a Woman.

A California judge has ruled that the 25-year marriage of James and Linda Corazinni was not legal. Linda had sued for $1,000 a month child support for their two children. But, said the judge, the evidence showed that James had masqueraded as a "husband" during the marriage. "He" was actually she, and the children had been conceived by artificial insemination.

Yet Another Amusing Bungle.

At the San Francisco premiere of *Coming Home*—the movie about the problems of disabled Vietnam veterans—the second-floor theater was inaccessible to handicapped persons.

Flying High.

The coach section on the National Airlines Miami-to-California flight was designated "no frills," but the 25-year-old blonde was in no shape to read. She came down the aisle from the first-class section with a champagne bottle in her hand, wearing not a stitch of clothing. Smiling happily, she climbed on top of a seat in row 27 of the DC-10 and settled down to swig the champagne, giggling all the while. She was celebrating, she told the enthusiastically clapping passengers, because she had just inherited $15 million.

A stewardess tried to put a blanket over her, but the woman climbed down and raced up and down the plane's aisles for 15 minutes as the passengers cheered the contest. Finally she was "captured" and led to a seat, where she conked out for the rest of the five-hour flight.

At Los Angeles after the plane landed, the blonde, reputedly a Las Vegas dancer, was led away by airlines personnel, but no charges were filed against her.

"She had a beautiful body," said one observant woman passenger later, "short blonde hair, a suntan all over. But she wasn't a real blonde."

✦✦✦✦✦✦✦✦✦✦✦

Fair Is Fair.

The monthly bulletin of the San Francisco Bar Association magazine notes that the association's Gay Rights Committee will be investigating "the extent to which homosexual bars discriminate against heterosexuals and other minorities."

A Civilized Divorce.

After 12 years of marriage, Gene Ballard, a 35-year-old carpenter of Concord, California, served divorce papers on his wife Lynda, 31.

The proceeding took place during a free-fall parachute jump from 12,500 feet. Ballard's lawyer handed Lynda the papers during the free-fall. Seven friends jumped alongside the couple as witnesses.

After Lynda had received the papers, the couple joined hands and, falling at 120 miles per hour, kissed goodbye.

Try to Picture This.

Police in San Diego were looking for Henry Leroy, who escaped from a local mental hospital. As part of his therapy, Leroy learned how to do macrame. He then fashioned a macrame jump rope, and at an opportune moment he skipped rope right out of the hospital. He was wearing his hospital gown at the time, as well as handcuffs and leg irons.

About Face.

The latest rage in Beverly Hills is Preparation H. No—not to cure hemorrhoids but to keep the face shaped up, eliminate those nasty wrinkles, produce tight, unlined skin. The famous Schwab's pharmacy and its branches report booming sales of the product, and many Beverly Hills ladies of fashion openly sing its praises as a face saver, claiming it shrinks pores and knocks out wrinkles— at least temporarily.

But Los Angeles dermatologist Dr. Jarrad Morris says that Preparation H on the face works by irritating the skin enough to cause a slight swelling, which presses out the wrinkles. Dr. Jaroff says that people using it are likely to develop inflammation and scaling, which will make them look older.

Asked to comment on the report of Preparation H's facial popularity, a spokesman for Whitehall Laboratories, its manufacturer, said, "No comment, particularly on this matter."

A Blow to Progressive Education.

A 26-year-old California schoolteacher has been indicted by a grand jury on charges of selling drugs to and engaging in sex with her junior high school students.

The investigation began when a deputy found the teacher hugging a young boy in her car. According to the indictment, the teacher gave her 14-year-old male students marijuana and alcohol, and had sex with them.

The teacher maintained she was being "persecuted," but the prosecutor said: "We still think it is a crime in this state for teachers to have sexual relations with their junior high school students."

It's Always Nice to Learn a Trade.

More than 300 students enrolled in a course on prostitution taught by Betsy Perry at the University of California at Los Angeles.

Euphoria Is an Endangered Species.

The Church of the Tree of Life in San Francisco has embarked on a crusade to preserve the several hundred natural plants that provide "highs." The church is concerned that psychoactive herbs are facing the threat of prohibition and extinction. Its creed is that people have a right to do whatever they want with their bodies, as long as they don't interfere with others. Those interested in joining this crusade can write to Church of the Tree of Life, 451 Columbus Street, San Francisco, California 94133.

2
Wonders Of Science

The trouble with science is that it has aimed for perfection in an increasingly complicated world. No wonder it's gone haywire in the process, spawning modern-day medicine men who actually believe they can outperform nature.

Back to the Drawing Board.

Gregor Mendel, the Bohemian monk whose work is the foundation of modern genetics and the theory of evolution, fudged his results, say scientists who have gone back to his original studies and found his data literally too good to be true. Seems Mendel gave himself the benefit of every doubt, made errors in arithmetic almost always in his own favor, and left out information that did not fit.

A Timely Warning.

The Maryland Veterinary Medical Association has warned that joggers who allow their pet dogs to jog alongside them in the summertime may be endangering the animals' lives. The association has received numerous reports of dogs collapsing and dying from heat stroke after running several miles with their jogging masters.

Medicare Doesn't Pay for Groceries, Unfortunately.

Thomas McKeown, M.D., of England's University of Birmingham is behaving like a traitor to his class. McKeown is convinced that health is safeguarded predominantly by how a person lives, rather than as a result of the "miracle of modern medicine." In fact, he declares, the belief that modern medicine can cure all is responsible for the ill health of millions of people who don't take good care of themselves.

The clincher in his argument, as McKeown sees it, is the strong evidence available that increased life expectancy is not the result of improved medical techniques but of more nutritious food, safer water, and better hygiene.

Right to the Moon, Alice.

NASA is selling cargo space on the first space shuttle. Starting in 1980, the shuttle is scheduled to make 487 flights over a period of 12 years, and NASA is reserving space in its 56-foot-long cargo hold for individuals, corporations, and institutions that want to send their very own cargoes on a trip into space. Each flight will carry eight such freight loads, which will stay in space for two weeks to a month before returning to earth.

This space travel won't be cheap: a 60-pound payload costs $3,000; 100 pounds costs $5,000; and 200 pounds costs $10,000. So far, NASA has sold 220 payloads to a motley group that includes large corporations such as General Electric and Bethlehem Steel; schools such as the Air Force Academy and Utah State University; and individuals, such as a beer distributor in El Paso, Texas.

The buyers have two major interests: one, to test the effect of weightlessness on various kinds of materials, and two, to test the effects of weightlessness on living things.

To reserve a cargo space, write Donna Skidmore, National Aeronautics and Space Administration, 400 Maryland Avenue, S.W., Washington, D.C. 20546, and enclose a deposit of $500 (returnable if you change your mind).

Forget about shipping off your non-favorite person; they'll be checking all the packages very carefully.

A Triumph of Knowledge.

Two scientists in Washington state have successfully cloned asparagus—which means, they say, that spears can be raised to identical size and picked by machine.

Grope Therapy.

Pierre Beaumard joined a course in group therapy in Dreux, France, because he suffered from obsessional fears and felt incapable of communicating with others—especially women.

The psychotherapist who was leading the group suggested that the 37-year-old Beaumard could be cured if he allowed himself to be sandwiched between two mattresses and walked on by four other participants in the session. This process, said the psychotherapist, would serve to "stamp out" his complexes.

Beaumard agreed and got between the mattresses. He was duly walked upon by the four. When the topmost mattress was removed, the group discovered that he had died of suffocation during the "cure."

How About Curing Poverty by Faith?

Rub them with a grass-hopper's "tobacco juice." Or with an onion soaked in vinegar. Or with the juice of milkweed or green apples. Or follow Mark Twain's suggestion in *Tom Sawyer* and bury a dead cat at the stroke of midnight.

These are some of the long-recommended folk cures for warts, and now modern science says they just may work. Skin specialist Dr. Jerome Litz of the Case Western Reserve University School of Medicine in Cleveland has become convinced that the most important ingredient in the cure of warts is faith. Litz treats warts with a "special wart tape," which is actually ordinary tape on which he pastes an impressive label. He simply tells his patients the tape will make the warts drop off—and most of the time they do.

All warts are caused by the same virus, according to specialists, and some medical men believe that "faith cures" work because they stimulate the body to secrete chemicals that fight this virus. The only recourse, if the faith cure fails, is to cut the warts off or burn them off using chemicals.

A Sign of the Times.

A bar owner called in New York psychologist Daniel Tortora to treat his six-inch-high Chihuahua when the animal became an alcoholic and began barking incessantly for créme de menthe. Tortora, who gets as much as $45 an hour for dealing with the mental problems of pets, dried the dog out, then gave it pills which cause vomiting when combined with alcohol. After a few miserable drinking episodes, the dog gave up booze for life.

The Healing Arts.

The problem of doctors' bad handwriting became so acute at the Kaiser Permanente Medical Center in Oakland, California, that the hospital hired an instructor to teach the doctors how to write better. Illegible treatment charts and prescriptions could affect patients' health.

At first doctors pooh-poohed the course, insisting that seeing up to 80 patients a day and writing diagnoses and prescriptions for each inevitably led to the degeneration of a doctor's script. But the teacher managed to inspire their enthusiasm for the course by coining a slogan: "Poor handwriting," she told her students, "may be dangerous to your wealth."

Another Item for Gloria Steinem.

Men and women respond quite differently when they walk in a strong wind, social scientists have concluded. Men squint and walk forward in an aggressive way. Women lower their heads and tuck their faces into their bodies when they are wearing pants, turn their backs to the breeze when they're wearing skirts. One theory has it that women's behavior in this instance is prompted by the desire to protect their breasts and nipples, since a nursing mother's milk flow will decrease if she becomes chilled.

Further Realism.

All infants who are not "within the bounds of genetic normality" should be killed at birth, advises Sir MacFarlane Burnet, an Australian M.D. who won the 1960 Nobel Prize in medicine. This is absolutely necessary to avoid overpopulation and genetic deterioration, he says.

The Two Wandas.

Wanda Marie Johnson lives in Prince Georges County, Maryland. She was born June 15, 1953. She used to live in the District of Columbia. Wanda has two children and owns a 1977 two-door Ford Granada.

Wanda Marie Johnson lives in Prince Georges County, Maryland. She was born June 15, 1953. She used to live in the District of Columbia. Wanda has two children and owns a 1977 two-door Ford Granada.

That's not a printer's error. There are two Wanda Marie Johnsons. The 11-digit serial numbers on their cars are the same up to the last three digits. Their driver's license numbers are identical.

The two Wanda Marie Johnsons were living parallel lives in neighboring communities, unaware of each other's existence until a series of medical-record

mix-ups, credit confusions, telephone calls from strangers, and a misunderstanding with the state motor vehicle department forced one Wanda to seek the other.

"People I talked to thought I was crazy," she said, and at first she began wondering about that herself. Each time she applied for a driver's license she was told that she already had one that required her to wear glasses. She has perfect vision.

"I had to speak to four supervisors before I got that straightened out," she said. A few days later, an automobile registration arrived in the mail. It was the other Wanda's. Her own followed in three days.

The two Wandas finally met through a newspaper reporter doing a story about them. After a pause, one Wanda asked, "What do I say to myself?"

You Can't Fool Mother Nature.

After 39 years apart, identical twins James Lewis and James Springer were reunited recently. The twins were separated a few weeks after birth.

University of Minnesota psychologist Thomas Bouchard will be conducting tests on the twins to study the effects of heredity and environment on their lives and personalities.

Meanwhile, he can ponder this evidence on the power of twinship: Both twins are six feet tall and weigh 180 pounds; both married and later divorced women named Linda; both had police training and worked part-time with law enforcement agencies; both claim mechanical drawing and carpentry as hobbies; and both named their sons James, in one case James Alan, in the other, James Allan. Family members also commented on their similar speech patterns, mannerisms, and postures.

+++++++++++

The Perils of Bullet Park.

Industry in the United States has come to the rescue of gun users. The Smith & Wesson Company is now marketing a nylon-clad bullet.

The company developed this new product because scientists have discovered that old-fashioned lead bullets can cause lead poisoning in the shooter. Fumes from smoking guns expose police and others to lead oxide levels four times higher than the recommended allowable dose. According to a research report from Mount Sinai Hospital in New York City, this causes dizziness, headaches, and loss of appetite.

Stress Test.

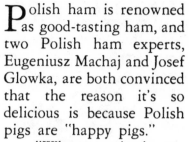

Polish ham is renowned as good-tasting ham, and two Polish ham experts, Eugeniusz Machaj and Josef Glowka, are both convinced that the reason it's so delicious is because Polish pigs are "happy pigs."

"When a pig is unhappy," Glowka told UPI reporter Sylvana Foa, "he undergoes biochemical changes that result in a high water content. It's what we call pig stress, and it's very important in getting good meat."

Machaj believes that Polish pigs are happy because they're fed only natural foods, like potatoes, wheat husks, and greens. "We don't feed our pigs chemicals and fish meals," he maintains.

Asked how you can tell a happy pig from an unhappy pig, Machaj replied that it could only be done "through experience."

Just like marriage.

But How Much Is a Dollar Worth?

The old cliché that the materials in a human body are "only worth 97 cents" is no longer true, according to Harold J. Morowitz, a professor of biophysics and biochemistry.

In his book, *The Wine of Life and Other Essays on Societies, Energy and Living Things* (St. Martin's Press), Professor Morowitz points out that inflation and scientific research into the workings of the body have contributed greatly to the enhanced value of humans. Ingredients such as hemoglobin and albumin are still inexpensive, at $3 a gram. But acetate kinase is $8,800 a gram, bradykinin is $12,000 a gram, and prolactin is $17.5 million a gram. Taking all of a human body's ingredients together, Professor Morowitz arrives at a price for a medium-sized human body. The figure is $6,000,015.44, which makes us all at least six million-dollar men and women, and may be the best news the obese have had in a long while.

Furthermore, Professor Morowitz declares, if you start from scratch to make a human, and figure in materials and labor costs, the price for turning out a slightly depressed, hard-working American man or woman is $6,000 trillion.

One Less Mouth to Feed.

America's canine population has increased by nearly 20 percent in the past five years, and that's why Carnation is now working on a dog food that contains a birth control drug.

The company considered 2,000 names for this product and, reportedly, has narrowed the choice down to the following: Extra Care, Chaperone, and Subdue.

Presumably, the drug will not affect male dogs, and, as for hungry humans, people who are so poor they have to eat dog food shouldn't have children.

Sabotaging a Growth Industry.

An unknown killer poisoned 200 laboratory mice, valued at several thousand dollars, by placing Xylene, a common laboratory cleaning fluid, in the bottom of their cages. The mice belonged to Memphis State University's chemistry department. According to a spokesman, five years of cancer research was wiped out as a result of the crime.

Back to Basics.

In January, 1977, Princeton University announced that it was computerizing its library's filing card system, at a cost of $150,000. The new computer system was supposed to give librarians instant circulation data and to check out books by means of a scanner system similar to that used in some supermarkets to check out groceries.

Today the library is back to using those old-fashioned three- by five-inch filing cards. The computer "tended to break down a good deal of the time," said a librarian, resulting in "records that were either scrambled, garbled, or outright lost," and many that were "totally false."

The library is looking for a new computer, but not too hard. The manual filing card system, the librarian said, is "exceedingly slow but most of the time reliable."

Disco Dentures?

Johnson & Johnson has patented artificial teeth that are fluorescent. The company was awarded patent number 4,170,823 for artificial porcelain teeth that glow fluorescently under ultraviolet lights just the way that real ones do.

3
Sex
&
Society

As everyone should know by now, sex has become *the* great creative activity of our time. Where else but in sex can the artist in us all give free rein to imagination, virtuosity, a flair for the dramatic, and a desire to shape experience into meaningful patterns? Is sex-as-art bad? Absurdly, it is if you're not good at it.

National Condom Day.

More than 1,000 persons of all ages and walks of life gathered in Union Square in San Francisco to celebrate the climax of the First Annual National Condom Week with a rock concert on a stage decorated with hundreds of red, white, and blue helium-filled condoms.

National Condom Week was sponsored by a coalition of sexual counseling groups and family planning centers to promote the idea that condoms are reliable, effective, and safe methods of birth control and to "polish the still-tarnished image of the rubber," according to Michael Castleman of the Men's Reproductive Health Clinic, the first birth control clinic for men.

The highlight of Condom Day was the selection of the winner of the Condom Couplet Contest, sponsored by the Population Institute of Los Angeles. Ten finalists from more than 500 entries were judged by Frank Zappa, Alice Cooper, Grace Slick and Janis Ian, who awarded a solid gold condom pendant to Ms. Jude Bartlett of San Jose for this two-line rubber rhyme:

"Use a condom and you'll learn

"No deposit, no return."

Just Trying to Be Helpful.

About 30 percent of all women who seek counseling wind up having some form of sexual contact with their therapists, ranging from kissing and petting to deviant sexual intercourse, reports Linda Daddario of La Jolla, California, in her 400-page doctoral thesis. The counselors covered by the study include psychologists, ministers of various denominations, and social workers. Of both sexes?

Enema Bandit Captured at Last.

Police ended the career of the notorious "enema bandit" who since 1965 attacked University of Illinois coeds and other women in the Champaign-Urbana area. Wearing a ski mask, he forced his way into apartments and administered enemas at gunpoint to his victims. None of the women was physically abused or otherwise sexually molested.

"Normal" Techniques?

The federal government is currently funding a $500,000 program to teach rapists the normal techniques of wooing women.

The Date of His Choice.

Paul Gilbert, 17, of Cumberland, Rhode Island, was refused permission by his parents to attend the senior prom with the date of his choice—another boy. He appealed to school authorities, but they supported the parents. *The New York Times*, in all its august majesty, disagreed in an editorial, urging that teenagers be dealt with "as individuals."

The Gong Show.

On a recent *Mike Douglas Show*, Zsa Zsa Gabor revealed some details of her married life: "All of my seven husbands beat me," she said, "and I loved it. I like to know that the man has the upper hand. I like to know that I make a man mad enough so that he beats me."

What's Wrong with Sex?

The Rosenbach Museum and Library in Philadelphia exhibited nude photographs of little girls aged 6 to 12 taken by Lewis Carroll, author of *Alice's Adventures in Wonderland*. The museum's curator, Walter Johnson, contends that Carroll was not a "conventional dirty old man" but that it is "impossible to deny the sexual nature of the photographs."

Marriage of Convenience.

Two male firemen in Alexandria, Virginia, one widowed, the other divorced, are considering marrying each other in order to make sure that their children by their previous marriages receive life insurance benefits. The system now permits only spouses to collect on the insurance of fire fighters who die in the line of duty. They are trying to get around that by marrying each other and assigning the benefits to the children. Authorities refused to identify the men, but said that they did not plan to live together.

Oi, Veh.

The 1970 National Nude Beach Weekend was not held at Playboy's Lake Geneva, Wisconsin, resort, as planned by the sponsors of the event. After invitations had gone out, the Playboy Club, which runs the hotel, announced that the nudist convention would be barred because it might offend hotel guests. Club manager Charles Dickerman explained the cancellation by declaring: "We're basically a family resort. Not everyone will accept nudity."

By the Numbers.

The United States Army has released a study which concludes that the main problem with men and women being together on the battlefield is "sexual fraternization." The report pointed out that romance between officers and enlisted women is a threat to what the Army terms "expedient mission accomplishment." As always, the Army's solution involves regulations and better training. It wants to set up guidelines that will delineate "unacceptable fraternization," and it wants male soldiers to be given training in what it refers to as "female physiology."

A New Deviation.

Long Jean Silver, an amputee from childhood, was arrested by police in Jamestown, Rhode Island, for using her stump to pleasure her friend Annie Sprinkle. Annie Sprinkle is the publisher of *Hot Shit #2,* an erotic tabloid. The layouts of *Hot Shit #1* were confiscated by the troopers as too obscene to print.

Instant Relief.

Dr. Jessie Potter, director of the National Institute for Human Relations, believes that sex can relieve the pain caused by arthritis. Dr. Potter, on the faculty at the University of Illinois and Northwestern University medical schools, told a meeting of the National Arthritis Foundation that sexual activity promotes the release of cortisone by the adrenal glands, giving arthritis sufferers four to six hours of relief from pain.

Machos Die Young.

Although women now live on the average up to 10 years longer than men, the success of the women's liberation movement may soon be shortening female life spans, predicts Ingrid Waldron, associate professor of biology at the University of Pennsylvania.

Some scientists believe that women live longer than men because they are biologically more durable, but Dr. Waldron says that the evidence for this theory isn't very strong; the real difference is in life style.

"In the contemporary United States, mortality is sixty percent higher for males than for females," Dr. Waldron says, "but forty percent of the excess is due to heart disease, which is more common among men because they smoke more." Other factors in the higher death rate among men are: using guns, drinking, working at hazardous jobs, and suicide. Men are generally under more stress than women and this shows in their death rate, she says.

In countries where the life styles of both men and women are less aggressive and competitive, life expectancies are more equal. Now that women are taking on male roles, their death rate may be expected to rise, Dr. Waldron warns.

Why Relationships Never Last.

Psychology Today magazine may have stumbled on one significant difference between the sexes. The magazine took a survey to discover the favorite leisure activities of married couples. From 96 possible choices, 45 percent of the men chose sex as the thing they liked best. But 37 percent of the women selected reading. For the women, sex just barely won out over sewing—26 percent to 25. Of course they're reading sexy novels.

Love Junkies.

"Romantic love" (whatever that is) is an addiction, and those who indulge in it—men and women—are hooked like dopers, can't kick the habit and keep coming back for more, no matter how often they're shot down. That's the conclusion of Professor F. B. Meeker, of California State Polytechnic University, who surveyed 105 men and women aged 18 to 43 whose love affairs had recently ended.

What makes life really tough for these addicts, says Meeker, is that most "sweaty-palm" romances are kaput after 15 months. "The half-life of intense romance is about ninety days—it decays like radioactivity," Meeker reports. But those surveyed remained unfazed. Ninety-four percent were eager to "fall in love" again.

One problem with Meeker's research may be a failure to define terms. Women surveyed were inclined to rank love as the most important element in a relationship. Men, on the other hand, said that sex was tops.

A Long Way, Baby.

Marilyn McCuster, 35, of Coalport, Pennsylvania, who filed a sex discrimination suit to get a job as a coal miner, became the first woman in the United States to be killed in an underground mine accident when a rock ceiling collapsed on her in a shaft of the Rushton mine in Osceola Mills.

Sin Is Expensive.

Arizona has passed a "living in sin" law making it a felony to be caught living together out of wedlock, with a punishment of six months in jail, $300 fine.

Hog Wild Wedding.

In Plainville, Connecticut, Mark Warner recently married his motorcycle. One hundred of Warner's friends attended the wedding, and then, reversing the usual procedure, the motorcycle carried Warner to the threshold of a cafe for the wedding reception. Groom and motorcycle exchanged piston rings after the ceremony.

It's Probably Better Than Valium.

The West German socialized medicine program has authorized payment of $10 per treatment for a citizen whose doctor and psychiatrist have prescribed six months of weekly visits with a prostitute for treatment of the patient's complexes and obsessions.

Common Sense.

Sociologists Elaine and William Walster have demolished the myth that most men are turned off by a woman who's easily available. Not quite true, they report in a government-sponsored study based on interviews with 431 couples. Actually, a man is most attracted to a woman who is easy for him to get—but difficult for everyone else.

Not Tonight, Dear.

Computer research into medical and matrimonial records indicates that, more often than not, those who indulge in extramarital affairs are subject to migraine headaches.

4
World News in Review

There are those who think that America has lost its way. That our country is prey to decadence. That our cities are a swamp of crime, immorality, and excessive behavior. They think, in short, that we have become a nation absurd. For their comfort—and as a public service—we present conclusive evidence that we are not alone. Absurdity runs rampant around the globe.

Lost and Found.

Amid much fanfare, President Ferdinand E. Marcos announced the discovery of a hitherto "lost" tribe of "stone men," living in caves near an extinct volcano in southwest Palawan. Marcos made a highly publicized visit to the tribe, and the news flashed around the world that anthropologists could study the ways of a people untouched by civilization and living as if they were still in the Stone Age. A week later, the Philippine government admitted that the tribe had been discovered by an American scientist in 1963.

Fortunate Weather.

A 37-year-old teacher in Aachen, Germany, out walking his dog, came to the assistance of a girl being attacked by three young men. One of the attackers tried to strangle the teacher. Another, seeing the teacher's tongue protruding from his mouth, sliced off an inch of it with his knife.

The attackers fled and the teacher was taken to the hospital. Police and firemen at the scene searched the area for the missing tongue tip. After three hours, they found it and rushed it to the hospital, where doctors sewed it back on.

Doctors said the operation was successful because the tip had frozen in the extreme cold of the night.

Are You Covered in Central Park?

For $12, residents of Hong Kong can buy mugging insurance as protection (of sorts) against the most common crime in the colony.

Is He/She/It a Republican, Democrat or Both?

In India, hermaphrodites, biologically neither male nor female but possessing both sets of sex organs, are worshiped by many as divinities, and sought after to bless a newborn child. Such blessings are considered vital to the child's future well-being, and unless parents cough up sufficient money and gifts, the hermaphrodite will lay a curse on the baby that, so it is believed, will make its future shaky in the extreme.

Chandra Singh is one Indian hermaphrodite who doesn't deal in child-blessing. Instead, Singh travels around the country as a kind of peripatetic entertainer who tells off-color stories. That's something he or she does simply for money. His or her main interest is in running for office, which she or he has done a number of times, without winning an election so far. Her or his chief support comes from women in the smaller Indian villages, who traditionally have revered hermaphrodites and lunatics.

Chutzpah.

On the Hawaiian island of Maui, a jeweler bought a ring for $100, not knowing it was stolen. When he later discovered it was a hot item worth $8,000, he thought of a way to catch the thief. He stuck it in his window with a prominent $15,000 price tag. Sure enough, a few days later, the thief was back in the store, screaming that the jeweler had cheated him by only giving him 100 bucks for the ring.

Called by the jeweler's assistant, the police marched in and nabbed the crook in the middle of his tirade.

Don't Be Ashamed to Ask Questions.

A shopper was lost for three days in a shopping center in Utrecht, the Netherlands.

The 70-year-old woman went Easter shopping in the multistoried complex and, she told police who finally "found" her, when she lost her way, she was too embarrassed to ask anyone how to get out.

A Curious Custom.

Snake is the featured dish in some 400 restaurants in Seoul, Korea. It is offered in many varieties, and diners are tempted by displays of pickled snakes in glass jars and by batches of live snakes slithering playfully in glass bowls.

Koreans believe that snakes are not only delicious but also good for what ails you, whether it's a depressed sex drive, a general feeling of the blahs, or a specific illness such as tuberculosis. Snakes are also renowned for their power to increase longevity.

A tonic of snake meat does not come cheap. A yellow python, whose health value is claimed to be high, will set a buyer back $400. And the rare, longevity-inducing albino snake can cost as much as $5,000, a price Koreans are willing to pay because of their firm belief in its proven power to lengthen the life of anyone who eats it.

Naked License.

Former Italian Parliament member and author Luigi Barzini urged the creation of a commission of beauty experts who would issue permits only to good-looking nudists and thus keep ugly people from going naked in public.

Banana Republic.

In Coacalco, Mexico, citizens who were furious at the mayor after police shot a local workman invaded the town hall and forced him to sign his own resignation. The mayor, José Ramón del Cueto, resisted, but finally signed the paper after he was forced to eat 12 pounds of bananas.

Duck Squawk.

Donald Duck is in big trouble in Finland. The deep-thinking Helsinki Youth Committee has decided that the Disney character is a national menace and should be banned. The basis for this charge: Donald's 50-year-engagement (that has *not* led to marriage) to Daisy Duck; the uncertain parentage of Donald's nephews, Huie, Dewey, and Louie; and the "indecent" barebottomed sailor suit Donald wears. These all add up to a "racy life style" that could twist the minds of impressionable Finnish youth.

Fortunately, Donald has a defender, a West German math teacher named Hans von Storch, founder of a 100-member Donald Duck Club (one of two in the world). Von Storch wrote the Finnish ambassador in Germany to protest this "ridiculous" decision. Donald, says von Storch, is "the most moral duck in history,"—doesn't smoke, drink or take drugs and "never has sex with Daisy," so obviously the Helsinki Committee's decision is pure duck feathers.

Utter Futility.

In London, grocer Mohamed Razaq was threatened by a robber who came into his shop and said: "Give me the money or I'll shoot you."

Razaq, an observant man, asked: "Where is your gun?"

The robber thought for a moment and said: "If you don't give me the money, I'll go out and get a gun and come back and shoot you."

Razaq made no move to comply.

The robber left.

He has not returned.

How Do We Know They're Really Virgins?

A secondary school in Brazil is now categorizing its female students as "virgins" and "nonvirgins." The idea is to keep these two groups in separate classrooms, in order to stop the long-standing bickering between the "moderns" and the "conservatives."

Prize Catch.

An Australian golfer, Noel Staatz, was playing on a course three miles from the ocean when he was suddenly hit squarely on top of the head by a falling fish. Onlookers theorized that the fish, a one-and-a-half pound mullet, had been dropped by an eagle or other high-flying predator.

The golf club's manager said that the fish would be stuffed and mounted as a wall trophy.

Why Poland's Industrial Production Lags Behind the West's.

A Polish sociology professor, Irenusz Kamelinski, who surveyed 10,000 Poles ranging in age from 18 to 65, concluded that lovemaking in Poland is far more romantic than it is in the capitalist West.

For one thing, says Kamelinski, his survey showed that Poles spend a lot more time kissing than Western lovers do, and they regard a kiss as a "more important symbol of intimacy" than the sexual act itself. The professor believes that Poles feel this way because they have been unaffected by capitalist pornography, which cheapens the sexual experience.

Finally, says the professor, most Polish men and women feel that lovemaking between 11:00 and 12:00 o'clock in the morning is the most enjoyable.

Sure.

Russian Professor N. Samsonov of Yakutsk University, on why Russian youth were wrong to yearn for blue jeans, rock, jazz, and other Western decadencies: "Take my word for it, the people in the West admire our Soviet fashion, seek out Soviet goods, love our art and literature, learn to sing our Soviet songs."

A Favorable Twist of Fate.

When Joan Campbell of Adelaide, Australia, found a wallet containing $225 and returned it to the rightful owner, the reward seemed quite modest: A 55-cent lottery ticket. It paid off with a parcel of beachfront land, a mobile home, car, boat, and trailer. Total: $45,000.

I Know What I Like.

In Karlsruhe, West Germany, an 89-year-old man promised the city a donation of $600,000 if it would commission a statue of small boys participating in a urination contest. With $40,000 of the donor's money, the city got a sculptor to make the desired statue. The octagenarian art lover inspected the work, said he didn't like it, and withdrew his offer to come through with the remaining $560,000.

Politics Is a Dangerous Game.

Citizens in Salvador, Brazil, recently elected an ocelot their mayor. Although the ocelot, which had escaped from a local zoo, did not campaign, it received 5,000 votes, beating both human candidates by a comfortable margin, apparently because voters thought that if elected it would leave them alone. It did, but they didn't. The ocelot was soon gunned down—by a disappointed job seeker, no doubt.

A Modest Demand.

Taiwan has announced that it is willing to hold reunification talks with Communist China.

Nationalist Chinese Prime Minister Y. S. Sun has stipulated one condition the Communist government must meet before the meeting can take place, however. The Taiwanese government will begin talks, Sun asserts, as soon as the government in Peking renounces its "Communist principles."

5
Police Blotter

Are we all criminals? Maybe. Still, some are more criminal than others. For them, the straitjacket of approved conduct has—for one reason or another—been too restrictive and they've stolen, cheated, defrauded, assaulted, and even murdered. Not surprising. But how do you account for the absurd lengths to which they've gone in committing their trespasses?

Objection Sustained.

Five cops in Orlando, Florida, had their photos taken in one of the city's topless bars. According to the policemen, they were looking for "clues" in the bar. But their chief didn't see it that way. He suspended them for 28 days and reduced them to the rank of probationary patrolmen.

The photograph showed the policemen holding magnifying glasses on "the evidence"—the upper regions of the bar's topless dancers.

Why Didn't He Shoot the Thermostat?

Richard Scalza, of East Rockaway, New York, was charged with reckless endangerment and criminal possession of a weapon after he and his wife had an argument over the temperature in their home. When Scalza suggested that the house was too hot and his wife refused to adjust the thermostat, he tried to force her to do so by threatening her with a .22 caliber pistol.

Too Busy.

An Illinois woman has been convicted of murder because she did not stop her boyfriend from fatally beating and torturing her infant daughter. The 17-month-old child of Pamela Ray, 17, was burned with cigarettes, beaten with belts and an extension cord, and scalded with hot water by Norville Hicks, 20.

"Most certainly this is a strange mother," said Circuit Court Judge John J. Hoban of St. Clair County. "She could have stopped the mistreatment of the child, but she was too busy watching television."

Tea and Sympathy.

Bank robbers have been grossly misunderstood, says Dr. Donald A. Johnston of the University of Colorado Medical Center. Contrary to popular conception, they don't rob banks after careful planning, but on impulse. And they do the dirty deed not because they want the money they'll get, but because they want to prove they can "do something big," because they suffer from feelings of inadequacy, because they are unconsciously inflicting self-punishment, because they are, in short, emotionally troubled and often psychotic characters.

For his report, which appeared in the *American Journal of Psychiatry*, Dr. Johnston talked to bank robbers paying for their crimes in the federal penitentiary in Springfield, Missouri. As proof that they more often than not act upon impulse, Dr. Johnston cited FBI statistics indicating that, in any given year, most bank robbers know nothing about the operations of the banks they attack, but simply walk in blind.

Among the cases Dr. Johnston cites to support his view:

The man who robbed a bank after he heard of the American moon landings, which made him feel "small and insignificant." He immediately went out and robbed a bank. He received 20 years for the crime, but doesn't regret his act. "I really did something big. It felt good," he said.

Two men robbed banks after they felt inadequate when they couldn't give beggars money. They set out to rob the first bank they spotted.

A lawyer with a wife and nine children who wanted to punish himself for an extramarital affair robbed a bank at which he was well known. He used an unloaded gun and waited for police to arrive. He then raised the gun at them. He was shot in the arm, raised his gun a second time, was shot a second time, tried to run and was shot in the leg. He told Dr. Johnston that deep down he wanted police to kill him because, as a Catholic, he couldn't bring himself to commit suicide—and also, suicide would cancel his life insurance.

A Victimless Crime?

A Brooklyn jury convicted James "Squeaky" Byrd of first-degree assault after hearing testimony from former prostitute Tina Young, 19. She said that Byrd, who was her pimp, punished her for talking with another pimp at a party by scalding her with boiling water, knocking her unconscious with a beer bottle, and then running a steam iron along her back and legs.

Beyond a Reasonable Doubt.

A motorist in Saginaw, Michigan, arrested for carrying a concealed weapon in his car, was released a day later when police discovered that the weapon, a pistol, actually belonged to the arresting officer. According to the police, the officer stopped the car and was searching it when, apparently, his gun dropped out of his holster.

Of Mice and Men.

V ito Poliseno, 53, of Howell Township, New Jersey, was arrested, along with his 20-year-old girlfriend and her two brothers, on charges of killing his wife of 31 years in order to collect a $50,000 inheritance. It turned out that the victim had changed her will, leaving him only $1.

Hot Panties.

A n estimated $100,000 damage has been caused in Redding, California, by an arsonist who breaks into homes, steals panties, and uses them to kindle fires, which, so far, have destroyed 10 homes, most of them occupied only by women.

The Fountain of Youth.

Ethel Mae Mottinger, 61, of Long Beach, California, was arrested after police found her daughter tied up in the back of Mrs. Mottinger's car.

The daughter, Charlotte Elaine Mottinger, was nervous and frightened when she was released, asking the policemen who rescued her whether they were going to drown her. Reassured, she told a harrowing story of having been held a prisoner by her mother for 20 years. Her ordeal began when she was 13 and her father died. Her mother then tied her up in the bathroom, starved her for days, beat her with electrical cords, a broom, a belt and, at least once, a soft drink bottle. When she was fed, her diet was gruel or rice, corn, bread, and water. Her mother warned her that if she told police what had happened, they would beat and drown her.

Police said that the 32-year-old woman looked no older than 15.

Ouch.

In San Francisco, a Korean sex therapist advertised that he could cure sexual frigidity, menopausal problems, narcotics addiction, and other complaints, including constipation, with his "golden needle" acupuncture treatment.

Venturing somewhat beyond accepted acupuncture theory, Pyong Ha Hwan Lim, 61, attempted to cure a number of patients by inserting needles into their sex organs. One woman ended up with 20 needles permanently inserted into her body, paying Lim $20 for each insertion.

Lim was sentenced to 14 days in jail, convicted of practicing medicine without a license and false advertising.

God Bless the Boys in Blue.

Police in Las Vegas put out an all-points bulletin on a man who was going around town kissing the toes of young women sunbathers. Ever conscious of the city's crucial role in protecting American moral behavior, the police called the toe-kissing a "lewd and lascivious act."

Is This Man Sane?

In 1971, Thomas Vanda was found not guilty by reason of insanity in the killing of a 15-year-old girl and put in a mental institution. He was released in 1976. A year later he committed a second murder and was put in Chicago's Cook County jail to await trial. He was expected again to plead insanity, but he may not be able to do that. Prison officials got hold of a letter he wrote to another inmate. Its title: "How to Beat a Murder Rap by Insanity."

The Razor's Edge.

In his trial for burglary in Toronto, Kenneth Sackville, 24, was described by a psychiatrist as "a female person within a male body." This condition, said the psychiatrist, created such frustration that it drove him to burglary. The psychiatrist recommended a sex-change operation, and after being advised by the judge to consider the seriousness of the operation and of the decision to go through with it, Sackville agreed to have the operation.

Hire the Handicapped.

Witnesses to a shooting on Chicago's South Side reported that Kevin Adams, 21, interrupted a conversation that Albert Stewart, 23, a paraplegic in a wheelchair, was having at a party. Stewart became enraged, pulled a gun from under his paralyzed legs, and shot Adams in the neck. At gunpoint he then ordered another guest to assist him down the steps from the second-floor apartment and fled the scene in his motorized wheelchair. Adams died several hours later.

Attention-Getting Devices.

Arrested for allegedly stabbing his wife in bed and biting off her nose, Eduardo Nedilskyj of Maywood, California, sat calmly in his cell and bit off the ends of four of his fingers, severing each digit at the first joint.

The Perfect Match.

Bobbie Ryan, 29, and Peter Hoban, 36, met through a Chicago computer dating service. On their first date, they had a few drinks at a local tavern, then returned to his house. Bobbie went to the bathroom. When she came out Hoban was naked and he began chasing her. His naked body was found in the bedroom of his burning house the following morning, dead of smoke inhalation. Police said that Bobbie left in Hoban's car and charged her with setting the fire that killed him.

Crime Doesn't Pay.

A 33-year-old man attempting to retrieve a purse stolen from an elderly woman in Brooklyn was stabbed by the mugger. As he lay dying, the woman said to him, "Why did you do it? I had maybe two dollars in change. That's all I keep in the bag."

The dead man was employed as an installer of burglar alarms. He is survived by a wife and two small children. They received gifts amounting to $17,000 in cash from well-wishers and are eligible for $9,000 a year for life under the New York "Good Samaritan" law.

Dope Notes.

Jamaican women in Montreal tried to smuggle $250,000 worth of marijuana into Canada by pressing it into long-playing records. Royal Canadian Mounted Police who seized 1,200 pot albums found they included a number of records with titles such as "Wages of Crime" and "Judgment Day."

A New Crime.

The French have finally decided that rape is "a serious crime." Though rape has long been a felony under French law, in the rare cases that ever came to trial, the charge was invariably reduced to a misdemeanor—assault and battery, "public leering," or some such evasion.

Ironically, in the case that brought about the change, the crime was committed against two lesbians. The two Belgian women, camping out alone on the French Riviera, were attacked by three men in their tent and, they charged, repeatedly molested sexually for four hours.

The defense argued that since the women eventually yielded, they had not been raped.

At the trial in Aix-en-Provence, supporters of the accused men threatened the accusing women, their lawyer, and spectators, at times physically attacking them as the testimony unfolded.

But the jury found the accused guilty and sentenced them to four to six years, as one more prop to the ego of Frenchmen—that no women can resist them—fell by the wayside.

Bad Doggie.

A Cliffside Park, New Jersey, man used an ax to kill a neighbor's Siberian husky that had escaped from its pen and was attacking the man's mother. He was summoned to court to answer charges filed by the Bergen County Society for the Prevention of Cruelty to Animals.

6
People

For all we know, there may well be a personality type, previously unacknowledged and scientifically unclassified, that can be labeled "The Absurd." If there is such a type, it can be recognized by the compulsion to behave absurdly; to think thoughts and perform deeds that are instantly identifiable as those of *homo sapiens absurdus*. What are those thoughts and deeds? Turn the page, please.

To Each His Own.

India's 84-year-old former prime minister, Morarji Desai, who is remarkably vigorous for his age, drinks a flask of his own urine each morning.

He attributes his good health to this practice and to a fruit-and-milk-only diet.

Desai maintains that urine-drinking is recommended in the Bible and is an ancient Greek and Hindu health practice, "a remedy for diseases in the human body provided by nature itself."

Who Wants to Take It?

Until he lost 900 pounds in 15 months, Jon Brower Minnoch of Seattle had the dubious distinction of being the heaviest human recorded in history, weighing in at 1,400 pounds, more than 300 more than anyone else known.

Minnoch became severely ill when he went on a crash diet of his own devising. He reduced his daily food intake to near zero calories, but the diet nearly killed him because, for some reason, his body ceased to eliminate waste. Firemen had to take a window out of his house in order to carry him, on a thick piece of plywood, to a waiting ambulance.

Taken to Seattle's University Hospital, the 38-year-old Minnoch was diagnosed as having serious heart, circulation, and respiratory problems. He was unable to move or to speak. He felt he was on the edge of death, when, suddenly, his pain abated for a little while. It was at this point that he felt he had been given what he called "a second chance," and he resolved that he would get down to a normal weight.

He is currently on his way to that goal, subsisting on a diet of 1,200 calories a day. Until he hits his target of 210 pounds, Minnoch refuses to allow his photograph to be taken.

Vampire Researcher.

Necrophilia correspondent Peter James Spielman took time off from the funeral directors' convention circuit to tell us about Dr. Stephen Kaplan, an instructor at the State University of New York at Stony Brook, who runs a "vampire hotline" listed in the Manhattan Yellow Pages under "Vampire Research."

"I'm often mistaken for a vampire," Dr. Kaplan told Spielman. "A criminologist is not considered a criminal, but for some reason a vampire researcher is mistaken for a vampire."

In his enthusiasm for his work, Kaplan has tried drinking blood. "There are people who have their teeth filed down to points and bite people on the neck to draw blood," Kaplan reported. "I have observed this and I've taken part in it. I've had an experience with an associate biting me on the neck. It was to see if it was possible for an ordinary person to nip someone on the neck.

"He didn't break the skin, but I did upon one of my associates. I was terribly successful. The person had the mark of the vampire and had to wear a scarf around the neck for two weeks. I drank human blood. It is a hot, salty, sticky red solution. I'm not thrilled by it, but there are those who are."

Investigating and publishing cases of blood-drinking is Kaplan's main

interest. He hasn't met up with any of the classic supernatural vampires, but some of his cases sought that goal—eternal life and youth by drinking human blood. There are, he says, Satanist cults that sacrifice humans (usually rootless hitchhikers) for their blood. For others, biting and blood drinking is a sado-masochistic impulse.

Vampires are always inconspicuous, Kaplan says. They wear business suits and casual clothing and melt into urban anonymity. Usually they restrict their lusts to consenting adult volunteers, almost always members of their own cult.

Kaplan thinks vampirism among consenting adults should be "permissible"—but sees no likelihood that this will happen very soon.

Dangerous Livers.

Japanese gourmets who eat blowfish, a culinary delicacy called *fugu* in Japan, are able to indulge their passion for exotic fare at the same time that they flirt with the great Japanese tradition of hara-kiri—ritual suicide.

Fugu, considered a great and rare treat, is eaten in special restaurants and can cost as much as $75 a portion. It is consumed raw, as sashimi, or cooked in soups or stews. The problem for the diner is that blowfish are poisonous, or, at least their inner organs are, particularly the liver and ovaries. In order to enjoy it, and tell your friends later how good it is, you have to be sure that you're not eating a poisonous portion. *Fugu* restaurants always have highly trained chefs who are skilled in preparing the fish, but it's not unheard-of for a chef to mess up and serve a deadly dish.

Tetradotoxin, the poison in blowfish, is 100 times more deadly than potassium cyanide, and each fish contains enough to kill 20 people. Since the poison acts in minutes by paralyzing the muscles, and since there's no known antidote, it's obvious that *fugu* eating qualifies as a high-risk sport.

The problem is compounded by the fact that, at certain times of the year, livers taken from a particular kind of blowfish are safe to eat—and the Japanese prize these livers above all other parts of the fish. So a careless chef or a tainted load of *fugu* livers can easily result in a *fugu* fatality.

Despite numerous deaths from eating poisonous blowfish parts, Japan's *fugu* fans remain true to their passion. But wiser heads have established one safeguard: In Japan, it is illegal to serve *fugu* to the emperor.

Please Pass the Finance Minister.

After Emperor Bokassa I of the Central African Republic fled his country, investigators discovered that one of the monarch's great delights was feasting on human flesh.

A large freezer at Bokassa's villa outside the city of Bangui was found to contain the remains of a number of human bodies. A 16-year-old girl identified her uncle as one of the victims. "His head, arms, and right leg were cut off," she said, "but I recognized him because of the tattoo on his chest."

The villa was used by Bokassa for private parties featuring "intimate" late-night dinners. Government sources indicated that Bokassa invited only his closest friends and advisers to these gatherings. According to one informant, Bokassa let it be known that human flesh would be on the menu when he told prospective guests, "Let's have some mutton."

From the Mouths of Babes.

It may come as a shock to the networks, but not everyone is a TV addict. A team of Canadian anthropologists from the University of Winnipeg recently came upon a group of Cree Indians in northern Manitoba who had never even heard of TV, much less watched it.

The anthropologists knew a perfect test situation when they stumbled on it, and immediately brought in a set to observe the effect of television on the so-called primitive mind.

The results? After a few days watching, the Crees told the anthropologists, thanks, but no thanks. They could go on doing very well without the tube. Their own shamans could summon up people living and dead, and those summoned —unlike the TV images— could heal the sick and predict the future. Besides, there were too many evil spirits on television, and these evil spirits invaded the bodies of their children and made them sick.

Finally, said the Indians, when you got right down to it, all the stuff they'd seen on the screen was boring.

Taking the Long View.

Recently a number of people and one computer were asked the same question: What kind of watch would you rather have, one that would not run at all or one that lost seven seconds a day?

Almost all of the people said they'd rather the slow-running watch. But the computer chose the stopped watch. It would be on time twice every day whereas the watch that lost time would be correct only once every 2,000 years or so.

How to Be a Big-Time Spender.

If further proof is needed that "the rich are different from you and me," British author Alan Jenkins provides it in his book, *The Rich Rich.* Among the examples he describes:

Sir Philip Sassoon once missed a train and immediately ordered the station-master: "Bring me another."

The third Marquess of Hertford never visited a huge estate he owned in Wales, but had dinner for 12 cooked there each night.

"The butler eats it," he said.

The sixth Duke of Devonshire razed a whole village because it spoiled the view from one window in his house.

Calouste Gulbenkian spent $2.5 million on a garden, kept 61 gardeners working on it full-time, and visited it only twice a year.

Jenkins' conclusion: "A true big spender is someone who spends unwisely but enjoys it. The element of pleasure is a must."

Love Taps.

The family-abuse victim of the future will be the battered parent, according to social workers, who are already beginning to see an astonishing surge in cases of elderly men and women beaten by their children in order to make them behave, change their wills, or turn over Social Security checks.

The Female Is More Deadly Than the Male.

Women are the victims in more than 85 percent of domestic assault cases, but men are the victims in 50 percent of all domestic homicides.

Standing Tall.

The next "in" slogan may be "Tiny Power." Incensed at such as Randy Newman's song "Short People" and many age-old insults, short folks are grouping together to promote their rights. In the San Francisco Bay area, a recently organized chapter of "Little People of America," dedicated to helping dwarfs, set up a basketball team called "The Stumpers." Its slogan is "Think Big."

Dishpan Hands.

An unemployed stockbroker was sentenced to 30 days in jail because he refused menial labor, such as a job as a dishwasher, that would have enabled him to pay child support to his ex-wife, a successful lawyer.

Donald Fanning, 43, now living with his mother in Sands Point, New York, was laid off from his $40,000-a-year position as a syndicate manager but kept making payments of $100 a week until his savings ran out.

His wife, Anne, who earns $22,000 a year, refused to discuss the case.

College Dropout.

Donald Stevenson Johnson may be the only graduate of Yale University who wishes he wasn't. Johnson has initiated a suit against the school asking Yale to stop "maintaining the disliked B.A. degree or any record of it." In support of his request, he said he "did not want" the 1945 degree in sociology and that a theme submitted in his name to satisfy requirements for it had been prepared "subversively" by his wife. A federal magistrate in New Haven, Connecticut, dismissed the case, noting that "cutting an old school tie is an unlikely judicial enterprise." Johnson intends to appeal this decision.

A Day to Remember.

During the 1979 gradu-ation ceremonies at Cedar Ridge High School in Old Bridge, New Jersey, 18-year-old Michael Matthews marched up to receive his diploma. When the school superintendent grabbed Matthews' hand in congrat-ulation, he was left holding it, because Matthews had inserted a fake hand in his graduation gown.

The angered superin-tendent then shoved the plastic hand down the back of Matthews' gown as the audience and the other graduates laughed wildly.

Matthews later apolo-gized, then explained that he had pulled the stunt so that he would remember the graduation ceremony. "Most graduations are bor-ing," he said.

Love Is Blind.

The widow of Nazi big shot Reinhard Heydrich says that he has been grossly maligned.

Her husband was being made a "scapegoat," she declared early in 1979, after the TV film *Holocaust* was shown on German television. "I didn't recognize the character they called Heydrich as my husband," Lina Heydrich said. Her husband, she asserted, was not an anti-Semite or a "monster," but a normal person. She didn't know anything about the murder of Jews: "Some were arrested, of course, but I don't know anything about the details. The Final Solution had nothing to do with my husband. That was something falsely attributed to him. The European Jews were all shipped to the Urals."

One of the most respected German histories of the Nazi period describes Heydrich as "the initial leader and organizer" of the mass extermination of six million Jews. As second in command of the elite SS, Heydrich was ordered by his boss, Heinrich Himmler, to set up and direct the "Final Solution."

Someone Please Explain This to Me.

Five months after she gave birth to black-haired, hazel-eyed female twins, Mrs. Rosemary Narimanian took the girls to a Philadelphia police station to have them identified. At birth, Maryam weighed eight ounces more than her sister, Shirin. Soon their weight became equal, but Mrs. Narimanian was convinced that Maryam was the slightly bigger of the two girls. "My husband kept telling me I was wrong," she told police, and finally she decided to get positive identification. Police compared the babies' footprints and discovered that Mrs. Narimanian's Maryam was actually Shirin.

Finally, Straight Talk from a Congressman.

The postcard to outgoing United States Congressman Mendel Davis of South Carolina was one of a series he'd received from the same constituent lambasting him for various actions and positions—in this case, his vote in favor of the Panama Canal treaties. Robert Payne of Mount Pleasant, a member of the John Birch Society, called Davis a "rotten skunk" and a "liar."

Davis replied as follows: "One of the small but gratifying benefits of leaving Congress is that I no longer have to put up with your unending drivel. I have instructed my staff to properly dispose of any future mail from you in the only manner appropriate to the content. Had any of your correspondence shown even the common sense of a gnat, or the simple courtesy one expects even of a small child, I would have been more impressed by your reasoning."

Payne said he planned to take ads in local papers reprinting the letter so that taxpayers would "know what kind of a representative they have in Washington." He also planned to write House Speaker "Tip" O'Neill calling for Davis' resignation.

Can't Get No Satisfaction.

A survey by the English magazine *New Society* indicated that most British citizens are not willing to work hard to get a lot of money. A majority of 1,000 adults questioned said that they only wanted to make enough money to have a pleasant life. Only one in twenty of those interviewed could be considered affluent.

On the other hand, when asked what would bring them the most satisfaction, a majority of the 1,000 answered: Money.

The Grandeur of History.

Pennsylvania's Merion Square Historical Society doesn't miss a trick. When Joseph P. Kennedy II, the eldest son of Bobbie Kennedy got married in 1979, in "the posh Main Line town" of Gladwyne, Jacqueline Kennedy Onassis attended the ceremony, and shortly before the wedding her limousine pulled up at a local establishment.

The historical society knew a good thing when it happened, and immediately prepared a three- by five-inch plaque to remember the event. The plaque reads, "This room was honored by the presence of Jacqueline Bouvier Kennedy Onassis on the occasion of the wedding of Joseph P. Kennedy II and Sheila B. Rauch February 3."

The sign commemorates Mrs. Onassis' visit to the women's toilet at Ray Utz's Arco gasoline station.

Prove It.

Twenty-five-year-old Ray Blazina and 17-year-old Bobbi Sherlock kept their lips glued together in a kiss for 130 hours, 2 minutes, and 17 seconds in Pittsburgh, Pennsylvania, recently. The old record, according to the *Guinness Book of World Records,* was 119 hours, and 12 minutes, set in Pretoria, South Africa.

While kissing continuously, one or the other of the two napped for short periods. The couple kissed while dancing, walking, or just embracing each other, although they pulled their lips apart for one five-minute break each hour. They did it to raise money for the Cystic Fibrosis Foundation.

Bobbi's boyfriend was a spectator at the event.

"We're not in love," said Bobbi, in the middle of their two-day-plus-long kiss.

The Dangers of Flight.

How dangerous is hang-gliding? In South Africa, sometimes very.

At a recent trial in Durban, Mrs. Loran Thompson testified that hang-glider pilots made lewd sexual suggestions to her as she sunbathed on the roof of her garage. Despite her complaints to the police, the hang-gliders continued to return to the scene and carry on their attempted seduction. And she continued to sunbathe.

On trial was her husband. The charge: Attempted murder. For the jury to decide: Can a man shoot down obscene hang-glider pilots to preserve his wife's right to sunbathe?

Underachiever.

A Miami woman was charged with beating her young son to death with her fists and a wire hanger. Mrs. Noorful Zulfa Dheen told police who arrested her that she became enraged when the five-year-old boy, Sajeed Dheen, couldn't recite the alphabet correctly.

7

The Automobile

It's not just a car, it's the emotional touchstone of our lives. We love it when it moves out smartly, feel castrated when it breaks down, hate it when it costs money, are proud of it when it's classier than our neighbor's. And above all, we exult in the power it gives us—over time, distance, and frail flesh. Speaking of the absurd, need we say more?

He Bought His License at Sears Roebuck.

On trial in New York City for the murder of Alonzo "Big Al" Johnson, Domingo Osario was accused by the prosecution of driving the getaway car, a late-model maroon Cadillac Seville.

Impossible, said Osario, outrageous, totally untrue. He wasn't nicknamed "Tony No-Arms" for nothing said Osario. In fact, he had no arms.

But policeman Michael Moran of the 25th Precinct disputed Osario's story. Moran told the jury that he had stopped Osario's car because he thought Osario was driving with just one hand. On closer examination, Moran found that Osario used the stump of his left arm to control the steering wheel and that, after the Cadillac came to a halt, Osario leaned over and turned off the ignition key with his teeth.

British Understatement Department.

Workers at the Vauxhall automobile factory in Ellesmere Port, England, celebrated Christmas on the night shift by getting drunk and tearing apart 50 cars. Three cars were too badly damaged to be repaired. The others were scratched, mauled, and dented.

According to company officials, the workers illegally brought liquor into the plant, began dancing on the cars, overturned two towtrucks, ripped up an office and, finally, stripped one worker and covered him head-to-toe with grease.

A Vauxhall spokesman condemned the workers as "quite irresponsible."

Getting in Touch with Her Feelings.

Police called to the home of Barbara Smith in King County, Washington, after reports of a disturbance, found a broken baseball bat and a smashed-up car in front of her house.

Upon inquiry, Ms. Smith told the law that she was responsible for the battered car, and then described how she had first shattered the windows and lights, then demolished the body.

"I feel good," she said. "That car has been giving me misery for years, and I killed it."

You Have to Love the Wrinkles, Too.

George Trammell of Los Angeles claims that anyone can get 200,000 easy miles out of an automobile. He had a 1941 Plymouth, which he won at an American Legion picnic for 25 cents in 1941, for more than 20 years. His 1966 Chevrolet has more than 166,000 miles on it, he reports, and it "looks and runs like new."

A 1971 Pinto is in fine condition at 90,000 miles.

The secret: Proper maintenance, daily checking of oil and—most important —lots of love. "My mother once said to me, 'You treat a car like it was a human being'," Trammel says. "You can love a car. I've loved every car that I have owned."

Don't Read This While Driving.

More than 10 million drivers in America don't have valid licenses to operate their cars. Many of these drivers carry licenses they have obtained illegally from other states after their own states revoked their legal licenses, mainly for drunken driving.

The problem is, says Minnesota Congressman James L. Oberstar, more than one half the states don't consult the National Driver Register, established by Congress to cut down on the number of illegal drivers by listing those whose licenses have been taken away.

Yum, Yum.

Douglas Elliot, writing in *The Co-Evolution Quarterly,* suggests that we start eating all the animals killed on the nation's highways. Carrion is perfectly safe when thoroughly cooked, he reports.

A National Tragedy.

Americans waste $20 billion a year on car repairs that are
faulty, needless, due to poor owner maintenance and
bad design, says Joan Claybrook, head of the National
Highway Traffic Safety Administration. About half the
total results from fraud or incompetence by mechanics.
The rest comes from increasing complexity of car systems
and owner ignorance.

8
Business As Usual

We take note here of a universal human phenomenon, the inclination of people and organizations to go on doing exactly what they have always done, even when the absurdity of their conduct becomes glaringly apparent. There is only one possible conclusion: Inertia is the root of all evil.

Discipline.

David Rhodes, 38, former manager of a Beaver County, Pennsylvania branch of the Century National Bank, was sentenced to three years in prison after a trial in which he admitted that he had administered spankings in his office to more than 50 late loan payers.

"I never had any trouble with them afterwards," he said—except for eight who threatened to report him to his superiors; these he kept quiet by giving them unrecorded loans totaling $88,268.

Rhodes, found guilty of misappropriating bank funds in making these unauthorized loans, said, "I didn't want to hurt the bank, yet I couldn't stop what I had started."

Next Question?

In the midst of a gigantic scandal set off by reports that executives of Kokusai Denshin Denwa, the Japanese equivalent of American Telephone & Telegraph, had been able to keep its rates excessively high by bribing government officials with gifts of cash, gems, cameras, and other valuable gifts, the company was asked if its $9-million annual entertainment budget was spent in bars, cabarets, and geisha houses.

"No. It was only for coffee and cakes," answered KDD President Manabu Itano, who has since resigned and gone into hiding.

What's in a Name?

The Hot Wok Chinese Cooking School of New York is taught by Norman Weinstein.

Getting Even.

Stealing by employees costs American companies billions of dollars each year and raises the cost of just about every product consumers buy, says the National Council on Crime and Delinquency.

According to a survey by the council, more than 50 percent of all employees nationwide steal from their companies. In some establishments, this activity reaches such proportions that it drives the company right out of business.

Only a small proportion of the thieves are caught each year, and despite the best efforts of security people, they continue to come up with offbeat and imaginative ways to rip off their employers. For instance, employees of a foundry in Buffalo, New York, made off with 129,000 pounds of lead by casting it in forms to fit their bodies, so that they could hide it under their clothing as they walked out. And tailors at a large clothing manufacturer were able to steal hundreds of thousands of dollars worth of material by minutely altering the patterns they were cutting.

+++++++++++

Yes, There Is a Faith Cure for Poverty, but it Costs Too Much.

A German-born Canadian psychic who calls himself Maha Yogi A. S. Narayana charges $2,000 a page for written reports on financial futures and demands a $10,000 retainer for foreign assignments. He says he's on retainer to two Wall Street firms and a $500-million Hong Kong bank and gets many assignments by impressing wives of company officers with his psychic talents.

Sponsoring the Imagination.

Science fiction has found a new world to conquer —the American corporation. The latest wrinkle in corporate planning is to hire science fiction writers as consultants who will introduce mundane executives to the far-out future concepts and thought processes of sci-fi. The corporations are paying stiff fees for this service, and an afternoon's talk by a science fiction writer can put $5,000 in his pocket.

What has prompted this trend is the corporations' realization that "future dreams" can be a rich source of new products and markets. The corporations are also concerned that their planners and executives are deficient in the kind of imaginative, innovative thinking that science fiction writers habitually indulge in.

Among the companies using sci-fi consultants are American Airlines, IBM, U.S. Steel, and the Weyerhaeuser Company. Isaac Asimov, the human writing machine who turns out several books a year, is one writer much in demand, but numerous other science fiction authors are now rattling corporate boardrooms with outrageous and unheard-of 21st-century ideas.

The Ultimate Recall.

In June, 1979, the American Pacemaker Corporation announced that the 552 heart pacemakers it produced might have defective transistors, and therefore might have to be replaced. All of the devices had already been implanted in the chests of patients with heart conditions. The company recommended that the pacemakers be removed from these patients in all cases where this would "be consistent with good patient management."

Objective Research.

As many Americans are now finding out, adding methanol (wood alcohol) to gasoline to create "gasohol" increases octane rating, reduces carbon monoxide gas, and gives better mileage.

Studies done in countries without their own oil predicted this was economically possible even before nations such as Brazil proved it with massive development projects. But research conducted in oil-producing areas was almost uniformly negative.

One of the few favorable studies in an oil-producing nation, the United States, was abruptly canceled by the MIT Energy Laboratory as "unscientific" after donations of $500,000 each from the Ford Foundation and Exxon.

Is This Boy for Real?

According to an editorial in *The Textile Reporter*, brown lung disease is "a thing thought up by venal doctors who attended last year's International Labor Organization meetings in Africa where inferior races are bound to be afflicted by new diseases more superior people defeated years ago."

American Know-How?

The leading category on the annual consumer complaint list is automobiles, according to the Department of Health, Education, and Welfare's Office of Consumer Affairs. Car complaints reach a volume more than double that of the second category. Other products and business practices on the list include: watches and clocks; automobile tires; mail order problems; appliances; business practices; and credit.

Glitch.

After a new program was fed into the computers at the International Business Machines Corporation plant in Essex Junction, Vermont, workers using the company's credit union began to notice large discrepancies in their bank statements. Embarrassed IBM officials announced that they were trying to straighten out the problem, which caused the credit union's account to be $1 million out of balance. They blamed the trouble on human error—and malfunctioning computers.

Hot Weather Housing.

Nudist apartment complexes are the latest thing in the sunbelt. These "clothing optional" developments not only permit tenants to wander around in the buff in halls, elevators, and gardens, but provide special shopping centers where the same uninhibited casualness is permitted.

Cynics note that while some staid citizens have called these developments "shameless," conservative banks, insurance companies and other "proper" lending institutions have been ready, willing, and anxious to invest in them.

Next Time, Get a Receipt.

The Del E. Webb Corporation, which operates gambling casinos in Nevada, allegedly spent $175,000 between 1969 and 1976 on female companionship for its gambler customers. The corporation says it has now discontinued this practice. One reason may be that the Internal Revenue Service disallowed $115,000 of this amount, which the corporation claimed as a legitimate business expense. The IRS noted that the ladies had failed to come forward with receipts for their services, and that, therefore, there was insufficient documentation for the deduction.

Braille Slot Machines.

Caesar's Boardwalk Regency, one of the new hotels in the new gambling mecca of Atlantic City, New Jersey, now offers blind people braille slot machines. The machines have a plastic strip on them that indicates, in braille, how the machine operates and what the odds are.

Highway Robbery.

At the height of 1979's gasoline shortages, the wife of an Amoco gas station owner in Freemansburg, Pennsylvania, was crushed between two cars in the long line waiting to gas up.

The station owner, Roland Amsellen, and the driver of the car that had hit her rushed to the aid of the injured woman. Meanwhile, dozens of drivers continued to fill their tanks. Not only did these motorists pay no attention to the accident, but only one person who pumped gas into his car bothered to pay Amsellen while he was ministering to his injured wife.

A Fate Worse Than Death?

In Iran, after the Ayatollah won power, one group of citizens that resisted the new ideals of the state was the country's prostitutes. In Abadan, for example, the bordellos were closed up and the women were directed by the Komiteh to hand over their identification cards and make themselves available to be retrained in a different line of work.

Not a single woman complied. Many began instead to walk the streets looking for customers and a number of them were beaten and raped. The prostitutes gathered at the Komiteh headquarters to petition for the reopening of the bordellos.

As one of them told an American reporter: "This is our fate. Do you think we are prostitutes because we like it? It's God's will and it is our fate."

The Dignity of Labor.

Everybody's trying to class up his or her act, which accounts for the following glossary of fancy new names for good old jobs:

○ Protective coating engineer = House painter.
○ Hair stylist = Barber.
○ Service representative (at car rental firm) = Car washer.
○ Mixer = Bartender.
○ Sales engineer, special agent = Salesman.
○ Security consultants = Private detectives.
○ Public relations assistant = Receptionist.
○ Sanitation engineer = Garbage collector.
○ Environmental control specialist = Janitor.

The Consumer Society.

Hotels are having a hard time coping with souvenir hunters among their guests. Besides ashtrays, towels, silverware, and other such mundane items, some travelers are after bigger and more exotic items. Guests have been recorded as stealing plants, doormen's braided caps, fire hoses, wine coolers—just about anything that isn't nailed down. And even that doesn't stop the more enterprising. At Hilton hotels, the management began screwing pictures to the wall to stop their being taken. The pictures still disappeared so the management began to secure them with glue as well as screws. Now the big problem is replacing the wallpaper that gets ripped off the wall along with the pictures.

Truth in Advertising.

J. K. Raimey, an Atlanta tire dealer, erected a billboard on top of his store, warning visitors to the city that its "police are underpaid, undermanned, and underequipped."

While the sign was being erected, parts of it were stolen by burglars. As the sign was being hoisted into place by a crane, a vandal severed the crane's brake lines. After the announcement was in place, thieves threw a brick through the window of Raimey's store, slipped inside and stole $5,000 in tires, wheels, and equipment, including a shotgun Raimey had purchased for defense against burglars.

Blazing Diapers.

Twelve tons of defective diapers being trucked to a recycling plant burst into flames in hot sunshine on a freeway about 20 miles from San Diego, destroying a 40-foot trailer.

It Makes Sense, So It Won't Happen.

David Brower, president of the environmental organization, Friends of the Earth, notes that each of the following steps could save as much oil as is contained in the Alaskan North Slope:

- ☼ Discontinue automatic transmissions
- ☼ Use only radial tires
- ☼ Achieve Japanese fuel efficiency in all cars
- ☼ Turn off all lights within ten feet of commercial windows during daytime
- ☼ Return electric motors to past efficiency
- ☼ Eliminate self-defrosting refrigerators
- ☼ Recycle motor oil

Do It at Home.

A federal arbitrator has said that it is okay for a company to limit the number of times its employees can use the rest room in the plant.

The limits were set by the Cagle Poultry and Egg Company in Macon, Georgia. The company apparently was concerned that productivity was suffering because of worker trips to the bathroom. It decreed that workers could only go eight times in a four-week period—outside of regularly scheduled breaks and lunchroom periods. That led to a walkout by the workers. Under the terms of the arbitrator's decision, Cagle employees are now allowed to go to the rest room twenty times in a four-week period.

+++++++++++

Cancer Is Good for You.

When a pesticide called DBCP, widely used by peach growers, was put on emergency restriction by the federal government because it causes sterility in humans and stomach and breast cancer in rats, the executive secretary of the National Peach Council, Robert K. Phillips, suggested that a better idea might be to look for workers who no longer wanted children or were already sterile.

"After all, there are many people now paying to have themselves sterilized," he pointed out. "Some might volunteer for such posts as an alternative to planned surgery for a vasectomy or tubal ligation, or as a means of getting around religious bans on birth control."

9
Halls
Of
Justice

Things go wrong, and often it's hard to set them right. Justice is a good word, but the wisdom of Solomon is in short supply. Should surgeons get back their old scalpels and sponges after they've been discovered in a patient's stomach? Why is life so complicated? The answer is, of course, absurd: Because it isn't simple.

Don't Complain.

Betty June Pelletier, a retarded person, was awarded $1.5 million in damages for being treated like a slave for 13 years. In awarding the damages, Michigan Circuit Court Judge William Beer said that she had been "treated worse than an animal. This is a shocking example of human serfdom." The judge awarded Miss Pelletier $1 million for false imprisonment, $500,000 for assault, and $55,000 as salary for 13 years of work.

Miss Pelletier, now 50, was released from a mental hospital in 1961 and placed under the care of Dr. Alvin Finch and his wife, Kathleen. The couple used her to perform housework, and she worked for 7 days a week, 12 hours a day. During this time, the Finches paid her $1,630, but forced her to sign the money back over to them.

In the course of the trial, Miss Pelletier described how the Finches beat and choked her and forced her to sleep in an unheated garage during freezing winters.

When she complained about their treatment of her, the Finches punished Miss Pelletier by making her pose for photographs with a chicken tied to her head.

Divorce Counselor?

Mrs. Penny Savader is suing her former marriage counselor, Nita Karp, for $300,000. Mrs. Savader sought the psychotherapist's help in solving problems with her husband, Louis. Ms. Karp advised him to move out of his wife's apartment, then urged him not to reconcile and then dropped his wife as a patient. Two weeks after the Savaders were divorced Nita Karp became the new Mrs. Louis Savader.

A Citizen's Arrest.

George Balboa, 33, isn't a lawyer, but he shows promise. Awaiting trial at the Nassau Correction Center on Long Island, New York, Balboa recently petitioned the court to conduct "a full grand jury investigation into the death of Joey the Mouse, my pet."

According to Balboa, Joey and he brightened their days in his cell by playing together. Balboa said he had made the mouse a cage from a cereal box and built him a cart to pull around. Sometimes he kept the mouse on a leash and walked him around the cell. He fed Joey, said Balboa, from his own prison food trays, and let him go for a refreshing swim in his sink. It was idyllic, until the day that the prison guards spotted Joey.

"What is that?" they asked.

"That is my pet mouse, Joey," said Balboa.

"It was," said the guards. "Watch how we're going to clean up your cell."

Cruelly and vindictively, said Balboa, the guards then dumped Joey in the toilet and flushed.

Telling this story to a judge, Balboa declared: "This is first-degree murder, a Class A felony, punishable by twenty-five years to life upon conviction. Joey the Mouse had a right to live and enjoy life, just like you and me."

The guards, said Balboa, "had no right to enter Joey's house without a search warrant and without probable cause to believe Joey had committed a crime." Besides the grand jury inquest, Balboa wanted the judge to order the warden to fly the prison flag at half mast for Joey.

The judge dismissed Balboa's petition, but some observers in the courtroom swore they heard tiny mice paws clapping as Balboa finished his presentation.

It Was Looking for the Garden of Eden.

Mrs. Ursala Beckley of Seaford, New York, set out to make herself a three-egg omelet, and as a result she has filed suit for $3.6 million in damages in New York State Supreme Court.

When Mrs. Beckley cracked open the third egg she was horrified to see a six-inch snake slither into the bowl. This experience, her lawyer charges, has made her "nauseous at the sight of eggs," and caused "a severe trauma" that requires psychiatric treatment.

An owner of the wholesale firm which allegedly supplied the eggs to Mrs. Beckley's local store, commented: "I don't see how a snake could have got into an egg."

Read This and Wince.

One of the most unfortunate malpractice suits on record was settled recently in Allegheny County, Pennsylvania, when 26-year-old Harold Michael won a reported $825,000 from a doctor who operated on him four months before he was to be married.

Further details were not available. The judge of the common pleas court, in which the settlement was reached, refused to comment further on the case, saying: "This matter is just too sensitive."

Michael's penis was accidentally amputated.

Be Careful Where You Sit.

Robert Rispler of Portland, Oregon, was having a fine time at an Oregon Oktoberfest until he walked into a portable toilet. As a result of his adventures inside, he is suing the Mount Angel Oktoberfest for $53,220. While he was using it, the toilet was pushed over by other revelers and Rispler was "violently thrown about," fractured his right wrist, suffered other "contusions and abrasions," and "became intimately mixed with the contents of said portable toilet."

Bare Facts.

The cute little girl with her pants being pulled down by a puppy in the Coppertone ad is the subject of a lawsuit by Jacquie Callaway of Idaho, who claims that it's her bare bottom and that the company therefore owes her royalties.

The picture is remarkably similar to one that her father took of her in 1946 on a San Diego, California, beach when she was two years old. The puppy is white, not black as in the ad, but he's pulling down her panties and the position of her body is almost the same.

Her father entered the photograph in a contest and won second place. It was published in the Los Angeles *Times* and a Canadian calendar company later purchased it.

Coppertone claims that the drawing and the picture are not related.

++++++++++++

Next Time, Reply in Writing.

Ruben Angotti, an Argentinian-born mathematics teacher, sued a local school board because it had dismissed him. The board said it fired him because his students couldn't understand his accented English. Angotti claimed he had been fired solely because of his nationality.

The judge hearing the case in Orlando, Florida, noted that, as Angotti testified, the court reporter had to ask him to repeat several statements. The judge called the reporter as a witness. The reporter testified that she did indeed have great difficulty understanding Angotti.

The judge dismissed the case.

Making New Law.

Mrs. Martha Burke's twin sister, Margaret, was killed in an airplane crash in the Canary Islands and, says Mrs. Burke, at the very moment that the crash occurred, she suddenly felt a burning sensation in her body, became terribly upset, and knew that something dreadful had happened to her sister.

This was not the first time she and her twin had experienced simultaneous long-distance pain. When her sister had a heart attack, she had shared the trauma, and each had suffered the other's childbirth labor pains.

Mrs. Burke has sued Pan American and KLM—the airlines involved in the crash—for $110,000, claiming that when her sister died she experienced extreme pain, and this pain was caused by "extrasensory empathy."

Only Fair.

Gary Braia of Redwood City, California, has been ordered to pay his estranged wife, Sandra, the federal minimum wage for her time when he is late to a scheduled appointment with her.

Braia regularly visits his wife to see their three children. Mrs. Braia, a nurse, complained that if Braia was late or failed to appear, she would have to change her own plans, hire a baby-sitter or turn down a proffered job.

A California domestic relations commissioner agreed, and ordered Braia to be on time or pay up if he wasn't.

10
The Official Mind

It hates logic, simplicity, spontaneity, common sense, and people as individuals. It loves power, regulations, duplication, complexity, titles, penalties, and people as categories. Its philosophy: More is better, even if it's worse. Its program: There are no solutions, there are only bigger problems.

How Much Did This Cost the Taxpayer?

Congressman Peter Peyser, of Westchester County, New York, instituted a new monthly award recently and made its first recipient the United States Department of Agriculture.

The department, he declared in a press release, had been wasting millions of dollars in overseeing the food stamp program, and therefore deserved the Peyser Monkey Wrench Award.

The trouble was, when he sent his staff out to buy an old-fashioned monkey wrench to send over to the department as a solid and graphic symbol of its dereliction of duty, the only one to be found had been made in Spain. This was just the excuse the Agriculture Department needed to send the un-American wrench back to Mr. Peyser.

Upon further investigation, Mr. Peyser's staff discovered that in America monkey wrenches have largely been replaced in plumbers' affections by a new kind of ridged pipe wrench. The congressman thereupon appealed to the American people, notably his constituents. "Help me save your tax dollars by sending me monkey wrenches," he pleaded.

✦✦✦✦✦✦✦✦✦✦✦

Put It in Writing.

A proposed law introduced into the Oklahoma House of Representatives by Representative Cleta Deatherage would require a man to obtain a woman's written consent before they engage in sexual intercourse and to inform her that she might become pregnant and that childbirth could result in serious health problems.

Experience Is the Best Teacher.

The fastest growing surgical procedure in the United States is the sex-change operation. Before 1966, according to one report, it was impossible to get the operation in the United States. Now these operations are performed in many states at the most prestigious hospitals.

Cost of the operation is from $5,000 to $10,000. Just recently, the federal government ruled that Medicare could pay for such operations, and that ruling will undoubtedly result in even more candidates.

The only requirement for Medicare payments, says the Department of Health, Education, and Welfare, is that the person having the operation must "have at least one year's experience living as a member of the opposite sex."

Is He Crazy?

Andrew Bavas resigned his $40,000-a-year job with the federal Department of Health, Education, and Welfare as a result of the commotion he created by attempting to refuse an automatic $1,272 raise. Turning down a pay raise is against Civil Service regulations, he was informed.

"Some people think I'm nuts for refusing the raise," Mr. Bavas said. "I've never been a very good bureaucrat. And after all this, I think it would be impossible for me to be effective in the federal government."

Why We Love Gerry Ford.

President Gerald Ford: "If Lincoln were alive today, he would be rolling over in his grave."

So Let It Be Written: So Let It Be Done.

If you or I put the wrong zip code number on a letter, it's no big deal, except maybe for the befuddled mailman. But it's a different story in Washington, D.C. Following is the Federal Communications Commission's correction of a zip code mistake:

"1. The U.S. Department of Commerce, Environmental Research Laboratories, has notified the commission that the zip code for its facilities at Boulder, Colo., is not correctly printed in sections 73.711, 73.1030 and 74.12 of the commission's rules.

"2. The city address zip code in sections 73.711 (c) (2), 73.1030 (b) (2) and 74.12 (c) (2) is corrected to read as follows: Boulder Colorado 80303.

"3. We conclude that adoption of the editorial amendment shown in this order will serve the public interest. Prior notice of rule making, effective date provisions and public procedure thereon are unnecessary, pursuant to the administrative procedure and judicial review provisions of 5 U.S.C. 533 (b) (3) (B), inasmuch as this amendment imposes no additional burdens and raises no issue upon which comments would serve any useful purpose.

"4. Therefore, it is ordered that, pursuant to sections 4 (1), 303 (4) and 5 (a) (1) of the Communications Act of 1934, as amended, and section 0.281 of the commission's rules and regulations, is amended as set forth in paragraph 2 above, effective Nov. 10, 1978."

Fire at Will.

President Jimmy Carter has confirmed Daniel Ellsberg's charges that American presidents starting with Dwight Eisenhower delegated authority to military commanders to start a nuclear attack "if necessary."

Ellsberg also says that the Joint Chiefs of Staff under Eisenhower secretly adopted a plan to hydrogen bomb every major city in the Soviet Union, China, and other communist nations simultaneously. It was called WARGASM and its technical title was SIOP for "Strategic Integrated Operational Plan."

Even Eisenhower was not aware of this scenario. Like John F. Kennedy, he assumed that he could nuke one nation without automatically bombing others. Ellsberg says that when he informed Kennedy and then-Secretary of Defense Robert McNamara about WARGASM they were "horrified." Kennedy is said to have changed the plan.

Said to have.

One of the major little-noted events of 1979 was a six-minute total defense alert caused by a computer error.

How's the Maid Service?

Inmates in Florida's 73 penal institutions are no longer getting a free ride on room and board. The Florida legislature in its 1978 session passed a law that requires all inmates with assets or Social Security income to pay $14.64 a day for their room and board. The law even applies to those who are awaiting execution. Prisoners who refuse to pay will not be eligible for parole. State officials have said that the cost of enforcing the law will be greater than the amount collected.

Do Those Mice Remind You of Anyone?

W hen he's not giving out his Golden Fleece Awards to those he says are wasting government money, Senator William Proxmire keeps a keen eye on other aspects of life in the nation's capitol. His latest concern is "the legions" of mice that live in the Senate Office Building.

"The problem has grown to epidemic proportions," said the senator. "We can no longer escape it. The mice are everywhere, and their size and numbers increase daily in geometric profusion. We have brown mice, white mice, soft, furry mice, short-tailed mice, long-tailed mice, fat, satisfied, arrogant, omnipresent mice."

Blind Faith.

Sharlene Sanders and Charles Lott are blind, and therefore entitled to receive a total of $502.09 a month in Social Security disability payments—that is, before they were married a few months ago. Their combined payments as a married couple now total $366.44 a month, reduced by their marital status, according to the Social Security laws.

The couple considered living together instead of getting married to keep their larger benefits, but decided they'd rather be married than richer. Said Mr. Lott: "If others want to do it, it's their business. I think they're going to have to answer to God for it."

At Your Service.

The average federal bureaucrat's wage more than doubled from 1967 to 1977, to a high of $17,400. After deducting increased income taxes and allowing for inflation, that meant an increase of $2,154 a year in actual purchasing power, according to Jim Davidson, chairman of the National Taxpayers Union.

During the same period, the average private nonfarm worker's gross income went up from about $5,300 to almost $9,600, but due to increased income taxes and Social Security payments this was a drop of $271 in purchasing power after inflation allowance, Davidson says. In addition, federal workers' pension plans are paid for entirely by the government.

Jesus Would Have Understood.

The New York Off-Track Betting Corporation celebrated Christmas by offering holiday gift certificates good in place of cash for bets in amounts from $2 to $250.

Stuffed Shirts.

Congressman Andrew Jacobs, Jr., of Indiana, is fighting a losing battle to convince his colleagues in the House of Representatives that wearing coats and ties to work is archaic in this jeans and T-shirt age.

The dress code, calling for jackets and ties, is for men-only in the House, and Jacobs has attacked it for violating the spirit of the Equal Rights Amendment. But so far Jacobs, who says he spends just $70 a year for clothes, hasn't made many converts.

When he appeared on the floor dressed in a sweater and open-necked shirt, he earned sneers, stares and, from older, stiff-collared members, determined shakes of silver-headed canes.

Why the UN Has a Big Budget.

In the course of a 1979 meeting, the United Nations Social, Humanitarian, and Cultural Committee considered a resolution it normally adopted each year, indicating its "strong support for the national liberation struggle against racism, racial discrimination, apartheid, colonialism and alien domination and for self-determination by all means, including armed struggle."

In the middle of the debate, the Thai delegate proposed that a comma be inserted in the text following "alien domination." Extensive debate ensued, during which it became clear that the committee members had no idea what difference in meaning would be achieved by the insertion of a comma. A vote followed. The comma lost, 17 to 38. Delegates from 61 countries abstained from voting, perhaps because they were awaiting further instructions.

Homework.

The National Parent Teachers Association has announced plans to spend millions of dollars to develop a program to teach students from kindergarten through high school how to watch television.

Suggestion Box Winner.

The Pentagon should start recruiting more stupid people, says Congressman Les Aspin, Wisconsin Democrat and member of the House Armed Services Committee.

Contrary to popular conception, Aspin maintains, the military services are not taking "too many dummies, but too few." The result is that "reasonably intelligent men and women" are being assigned to many military jobs that much stupider individuals could handle. This lowers morale, and the way to handle the problem, Aspin insists, is in effect, to put morons in moronic jobs.

Neither Rain nor Snow.

Postal inspectors found 10,000 pieces of mail stashed away in the garage of a Michigan mailman. The discovery came after numerous complaints from residents along the man's route.

Miles Ginter, a Grand Rapids postal inspector, explained that the delinquent deliverer had not tried to open the letters but simply dumped them in the garage. He said that the postman, who had been on the job for five years, told him the work had become too difficult. "He told me he just couldn't handle it anymore, " Ginter said.

Poor Practice.

When radioactivity was discovered in the drinking fountains at a nuclear power plant, investigators traced the contamination to a 3,000-gallon radioactive waste tank that had been connected by mistake to the water supply. Their report concluded: "The coupling of a contaminated system with a potable water system is considered poor practice in general."

Evil Is Winning.

The men and women who devise and execute American foreign policy see themselves as Luke Skywalkers and, like that *Star Wars* good guy, are dedicated to defeating evil wherever it crops up in the world. That's the conclusion of Lloyd Etheredge, reached after a seven-year study of America's foreign policy personnel.

An MIT social psychologist, Etheredge was amazed at the "heroic fantasies" held by the men and women he studied. "They see themselves as striving, grandiose, aggressive, defeating evil." This attitude, he noted, has led to an American tendency to use force, but also to a foreign policy based on benevolence and paternalism.

Etheredge cites John F. Kennedy as an example of the type, a man who read James Bond, wrote *Profiles in Courage,* set up the hard-hitting, fast-action Green Berets, and supported the Bay of Pigs invasion that would rescue Cuba from Communist evil, his "entire fantasy life displaced on foreign policy."

In the course of his study, Etheredge discovered that Foreign Service officers generally had a strong inclination to project their own personality traits onto foreign leaders and foreign countries. Peace-minded individuals viewed other countries as unaggressive. Hawks were convinced the whole world was full of aggressive nations out to get the United States.

Like Unto Like.

Homosexual teenage foster children are now being placed with lesbian couples by the New Jersey Department of Human Services.

Fat Chance.

The Taj Mahal is being eaten up by pollution, according to a recent government report. The report noted that the building, often called the most beautiful in the world, is now surrounded by two power plants, 250 iron foundries, and a railroad yard. The structure was built in the 17th century as a tribute to an Indian monarch's devotion to his wife.

The report recommended that the foundries, the power plants, and the railroad yard be moved to protect the monument.

No Concealed Weapons.

Authorities at the Wisconsin State Prison refused to deliver a copy of *The Progressive* magazine to one of the inmates because the magazine contained an article on how to make a hydrogen bomb. (The federal government had tried unsuccessfully to prevent *The Progressive* from publishing the article.)

Returning the magazine, a prison official noted that the article presented "a probable hazard to the peace, order, and safety of the institution and the inmate."

Erwin Knoll, *The Progressive*'s editor, expressed doubt that the inmate would have been able to acquire the billions of dollars necessary to produce the hydrogen bomb, and, if he had, whether he would have then found it possible "to construct in his cell the huge industrial complex" needed to make the superweapon.

Come and Get 'Em.

In the interest of maintaining staff morale in the face of cuts in the number of titles available to important Federal Energy Administration personnel, a memo was issued by Leonard B. Pouliot, Assistant Administrator, Management and Administration, announcing that the following could be awarded in the next two weeks: Deputy Assistant Associate Administrator, Assistant Deputy Associate Administrator, Associate Assistant Deputy Administrator, and Associate Deputy Assistant Administrator. Title requests were to be directed to the Deputy Associate Assistant Administrator for Management Nomenclature.

11
Whistle-Blowers

Whistle-blowing may be on its way to respectability. In the past, despite (or because of) the headlines they've generated, whistle-blowers have often been demeaned, demoted, or dismissed. But with growing public awareness of the outrages perpetrated by corporate profit-hounds and bureaucratic boneheads, those who have the guts to expose corporate and political inanities are getting publicity and praise.

The Golden Fleece.

The Muhammad Ali of whistle-blowers is Wisconsin's Senator William Proxmire.

What do you do if you're the target of this arch-foe of ridiculous government spending? Often you fight back, and make matters worse. One of Proxmire's recent Golden Fleece awards for wasting taxpayers' money went to the National Institute of Mental Health because the institute had spent $97,000 on research on tribes in the Peruvian Andes. For this money, said Proxmire, the taxpayers got an article investigating a Peruvian brothel. Among the article's choicer quotes, dwelt on lovingly by the senator: "By visiting the brothel at various times, it was possible to obtain a good idea of its everyday functioning."

The $97,000 grant went to Dr. Pierre L. van den Berghe, of the University of Washington, and his associate, Dr. George Primov. Van den Berghe fought back, defending the grant and the article, saying it was just one of more than a dozen papers the team had produced. The brothel article was Primov's idea, and, said van den Berghe, "It's something he did mostly in the evenings."

Proxmire himself remained silent when he was attacked by the Young Americans for Freedom, which awarded him a Tarnished Fleece for his efforts to get the United States Agriculture Department to fund a Dairy Forage Research Center at the University of Wisconsin. The center would cost $10 million to set up, and $2 million yearly, all for the purpose, said the YAF, of "studying what cows eat."

Strontium 90, Humans 0.

Despite nearly 6,000 studies, no permanent safe storage or disposal method for nuclear waste has been achieved, the late Congressman Leo J. Ryan charged in one of his last statements as chairman of the Environment, Energy, and Natural Resources Subcommittee of the House Committee on Government Operations.

A total of 74.6 million gallons of high level radioactive waste has been placed in temporary storage since 1944 in steel drums that have an estimated life of twenty years. So far, nearly 500,000 gallons have leaked into our water supplies from 1958 to 1975. One leak at the Department of Energy's Hanford, Washington, plutonium production plant went unnoticed for 48 days.

Although the Department of Energy claims that the Hanford storage tanks are safe, radioactivity is moving downward toward the Columbia River, ac-

cording to George Debuchananne, chief of the Office of Radiohydrology of the United States Geologic Survey.

Commercial low-level radioactive waste dumping has occurred at six sites in the United States. Of these, four are leaking radioactivity into underground water on the site, with those at West Valley, New York, and Maxey Flats, Kentucky, leaking directly into the local watersheds. One of the still-dry sites, at Beatty, Nevada, has a pilferage problem. The other, at Hanford, recently opened.

Because of the government's failure to find a safe way of dealing with nuclear waste, 3,000 metric tons of spent fuel rods are being stored temporarily at commercial power sites in "swimming pools"—concrete tanks filled with water to keep the rods cool.

An additional 145,000 tons of high-level radioactive spent fuel will accumulate by the year 2000, based on existing and planned nuclear plants.

There are now 67 plants in operation in the United States, 89 under construction, and 76 planned. Ryan's committee estimates that even if it were feasible to store existing waste with current technology, it would cost $75 billion. But the cost of dealing with waste has not been figured into the costs of the nuclear power facilities built or under construction.

"The nuclear industry itself estimates it will run out of even temporary storage space by 1985," Ryan said. "An additional seventeen thousand metric tons of nuclear waste will pile up in the next ten years. A recent Energy Research and Development Administration study says lack of storage space may force shutdown of twenty-three nuclear plants. Yet the Department of Energy and the Nuclear Regulatory Commission continue to claim that a solution exists.

"When I inspected the nuclear dump at Sheffield, Illinois, in the middle of the Mississippi River watershed, all I could ask was, 'Who allowed this to happen?'"

✤

Editor's Note: The question is the subject of a lawsuit by the State of Illinois against the California-based Nuclear Engineering Company, a private company which leases the Sheffield site and operates the dump. Nuclear waste disposal in Illinois was authorized by an act of legislature, under which the facility was approved by the state health department. Franklin Yoder was director at the time. He says, "It was recommended to me. I approved it. I take full responsibility. I have received no information that leads me to believe it was a bad decision." Mr. Yoder is now head of the Weld County Health Department in Colorado.

Nuclear Horror.

A defect in the manufacture of a $50 relay in any one of the nuclear power plants now operating in the United States could cause an explosion that would poison 500,000 square miles—*an area equal to half the land east of the Mississippi*—for three to thirty years.

That warning—issued years before Three Mile Island—came from Richard E. Webb, a former Atomic Energy Commission engineer who was responsible for the reactor in the nation's first commercial nuclear power station at Shippingport, Pennsylvania.

"It doesn't have to be a relay," Webb explained. "It could be a fluke short circuit, an electrical fire in a control system, many different kinds of human errors. All of these things have happened and will continue to happen. We have had many near misses. The next one could be the big one."

Author of *The Accident Hazards of Nuclear Power Plants* (University of Massachusetts Press, 1976), Webb said that in the event of a major explosion no food could be grown in the affected area for at least 3 years and it might take 30 years for the land to recover. About 125,000 square miles would be unsafe for human life for at least 2 years. The plume of radioactive smoke would be 75 miles long and a mile wide. It would kill everyone it touched.

Webb dismissed government studies of nuclear power safety as mere "conjecture" based only on computer simulations. Large-scale experiments involving the destruction of full-sized reactors may be necessary, he said, but reports by atomic energy industry scientists recommending this as early as 1964 have been kept secret.

Cut off from all official research funds, Webb was also dumped by the anti-nuclear power establishment in the U.S., which preferred to concentrate on the more respectable nuclear waste disposal issue. At one point, evicted from their home, Webb and his wife and two children slept on the floor of the University of Massachusetts office.

Webb's reports have been used to fight the construction of a nuclear power plant in Kalkar, Germany. A German appeals court ruled against the plant. The case now goes to the German Supreme Court for a final decision.

Troublemaker.

Serving a two-year sentence for violating probation on a $35 bad-check conviction, Jim Maslinski broke the convicts' code when he testified against three men he discovered raping an 18-year-old boy in a prison shower room. In order to protect him, the Florida Department of Corrections began transferring Maslinski from prison to prison, but he was threatened with death, stabbed, burned, and beaten at nearly every stop. Finally, he escaped, married, and took a job. He was arrested in West Palm Beach and held without bond in the Broward County Jail, where he is in danger again. Mr. Maslinski said that most prison officials ignored his pleas for help. Some who tried to protect him, however, put him in isolation cells normally used for troublemakers.

Score One for Science.

Although breast-feeding produces healthier babies, mothers' milk concentrates so many toxic chemicals, such as pesticides from the environment, that many groups that were strongly against bottle-feeding are now beginning to believe that in some areas it may actually be safer than nursing.

Our Vanishing Land.

Land is dying so rapidly throughout the world that major famines are inevitable within the next 20 years and there may be no way to reverse the trend, reports Erik P. Eckholm of the Worldwatch Institute, an economic research organization located in Washington, D.C.

About 43 percent of the earth's land is now desert or semi-desert. In the United States, a recent survey of public lands controlled by the Bureau of Land Management revealed that 50 million acres—an area equal to Utah—are in poor or bad condition.

Throughout the world, Eckholm says, mountains are being stripped of trees faster than new ones can be planted. Farmlands are requiring more and more chemical fertilizers but producing less food. Already, one-third of the world's population is running out of food and fuel.

Minor changes in weather patterns, such as the recent droughts, or decreased availability of fertilizers made from petroleum could produce disaster, Eckholm warns.

"The United States has been lucky so far," he says, "but if we don't change our patterns of land use and begin planting trees instead of cutting them down, we're going to have a total breakdown that will dwarf the dust storms of the Thirties—and maybe it's already too late."

Nerve Gas Alert.

Despite protests from the Governor of Utah, the Army plans to continue shipping deadly nerve gas to a depot thirty miles from Salt Lake City built in an active earthquake zone.

According to Governor Scott M. Matheson, the Tooele Army Depot already contains enough nerve gas to kill the entire population of the world 42 times over. It is contained in concrete "igloos" located along a series of geologic faults. The region has a history of earthquakes of up to 5.1 on the Richter scale. The Army claims that Tooele is safe up to 7.5 Richter and that the probability of an earthquake that strong is once every 12,000 to 30,000 years.

Governor Matheson believes that the gas is so dangerous that it should all be neutralized immediately wherever it is located. The Defense Department agreed to do so in 1972, but apparently has made no moves toward actually getting rid of the gas yet. Defense Secretary Harold Brown has approved the shipment of several tons of "Weteye" nerve gas artillery shells to Tooele. This is the newest and most deadly form of the poison gas. The contents of one shell can destroy life in thousands of square miles.

Nerve gas is odorless, tasteless and invisible. It kills in 14 seconds. There is no known antidote.

Running in Place.

Arms control talks between the United States and Russia speed up the arms race rather than slowing it down, says Cornell University professor of nuclear physics, Jay Orear.

"The basic fact of arms control negotiations is that neither side gives up significant points," Orear says. "The whole thing is just a public relations show for media. When they do agree not to produce a particular weapons system it's because they've already decided it won't work or it will cost too much."

Orear says that both governments spend billions of dollars on unnecessary weapons solely for the purpose of making the negotiations look real. "We spent a couple of billion dollars building an anti-ballistic-missile base in Utah as a bargaining chip to use in the arms control poker game," he says. "Another case like that was the B-1 bomber."

While one side or the other trades off trivial weapons, the really dangerous systems are allowed to slide through quietly, Orear warns. "In the current negotiations," he points out, "Russia and the United States have agreed to use cruise missiles. This single weapon is probably bringing us closer to nuclear war than all the others combined."

"A cruise missile costs only $1 million," he says. "In the game we're in, that's a supermarket item. The Air Force wants six thousand of them. They're like the old World War II German buzz bombs. They have a lightweight, air breathing, simple engine and a minicomputer that will put them down the hole of a Minuteman silo at five thousand miles.

"They're so cheap you fire them in volleys of hundreds at a time, like artillery shells. They fly at tree-top level below the radar network. Even if fewer than half get through, you can wipe out an entire superpower's defense system.

"The worst part is that anyone can afford them. Before long the United States will have every single town in Russia targeted with a cruise missile with a nuclear warhead. And the Russians will have every town in the United States down to Plains, Georgia, pinpointed. At least we'll know about those. But what will we do about the ones that Qaddafi or South Yemen have?"

Is Nothing Sacred?

The official figure for the American gross national product is mostly political hot air, says George Cruikshank, of the Morgan Guaranty Bank Economic Newsletter.

The gross national product is the total dollar value of all a country's goods and services, officially about $1.9 trillion for 1977 in the United States.

Cruikshank maintains that most of the supposed GNP increase in the past 30 years has been due to inflation. If the figure were given in 1946 dollars, it would be only $590 billion. And even that figure is questionable, in Cruikshank's view, since the GNP measures business activity, rather than prosperity or growth. "If you have an automobile accident and wind up in the hospital, the cost is added to the gross national product. The GNP ignores the damage that a bulldozer may do to the land and it doesn't measure truly important contributions to the economy such as work done by housewives."

Cruikshank's conclusion: Even though the GNP has grown about 3.5 percent a year in real dollars since 1946, it might be considerably smaller if the values destroyed by negative activities were subtracted.

Impotence Epidemic.

An epidemic of impotence is hitting male workers in the chemical industry, reports Anthony Mazzocchi, vice-president of the Oil, Chemical, and Atomic Workers Union.

Most of the reported cases are in plants manufacturing diethylstilbestrol (DES), a hormone added to cattle feed to produce faster fattening.

The hormone, once given to women as a "morning after" birth control pill, has also been associated with cancer of the cervix in their offspring.

Mazzocchi says that the drug is causing breast cancer in men and that a number of workers have had to have breasts removed; in one case, both breasts. He believes that more impotence exists than is being reported.

"This is a very sensitive subject," he says. "The guys don't want to talk about it. But a group of women get together and somehow they start talking about their sexual problems and they realize that their guys all work in the same plant."

Although the most obvious cases are coming from the DES plants, Mazzocchi believes that many cases of impotence diagnosed as psychological in the past actually may have been caused by exposure to various toxic chemicals.

"American industry is grabbing workers by the balls," he says. "All of the reproductive organs are being assaulted. We are hurting generations as yet unborn with genetic damage that we can only guess at now."

12
Paranoia
Patrol

These items are here to evoke the sensation of paranoia. There is something absurd about paranoia, especially the feeling of being tricked—both during an episode, and afterward in the embarrassment of reality. We cherish our paranoias because they make us feel important when we are in their grip— and because we feel like fools when we have to give them up.

Taking No Chances.

Countries around the world will spend nearly a million dollars every minute on war weapons. The total comes to more than $400 billion, more than half of this expended by the United States and the Soviet Union.

The U. S. and Russia together possess nuclear weapons with a combined total explosive power of 32 trillion pounds of explosives, the equivalent of 4 tons of TNT for every man, woman, and child on the earth, or, calculated in another way, enough explosives to sprinkle each of the 400 largest cities in the northern hemisphere with 2,000 Hiroshima-sized atomic bombs.

Meanwhile, arms spending is called the single greatest factor in inflation by many economists. It removes assets from general use and concentrates them in nonproductive, expensive, and dangerous uses, thus reducing the world's real wealth—reflected in the declining value of currency.

What Does This Do to the Work Ethic?

Salaries in America could hit astronomic levels, if the soaring inflation rate continues. Economists polled by the *Chicago Tribune* estimated that in 30 years, at a 10 percent-a-year inflation rate, a worker making $10,000 now would have to paid $100,000 in order for his salary to keep up with prices. And even that amount would not make workers better off than they are today: They'd be in a higher tax bracket and pay more in taxes.

More Realism.

A majority of children asked to choose between their fathers and television chose television.

Test Yourself for Cancer.

If you were emotionally upset as a child but repressed unpleasant experiences and found it difficult to get angry, and if you now think of yourself as healthy, even-tempered, and ready to cope with life, you are a typical potential cancer patient, according to Professor Claus Bahnson, a psychiatrist at Thomas Jefferson University in Philadelphia.

Going further, Bahnson suggests that women who lived in conflict with their mothers, who resent sex, and who have difficulty accepting their roles as females are particularly prone to breast cancer.

Bahnson believes that in 5 or 10 years, doctors will, through psychological testing, be able to pick out as many as 70 percent of cancer victims.

America the Free?

The United States has a higher proportion of its population in jail than any nation in the world, according to a study by criminologist Eugene Doleschal. Our rate of 215 inmates per 100,000 persons is going up, he reports, and the average American sentence is the world's highest, with the exception of political sentences in South Africa, Russia, South Korea and some countries in Latin America. The U. S. rate of imprisonment is 12 times higher than in Holland, which has the world's lowest—18 per 100,000.

The Pursuit of Happiness.

There are counties in Mississippi that have a higher infant mortality rate than Calcutta.

Don't Be a Hero.

When a skunk became trapped in an irrigation pipe in Colts Neck, New Jersey, three public-spirited citizens tried to go to its rescue. They lifted up the 40-foot aluminum pipe in order to free the animal. Two of the men were killed when the pipe struck a high-voltage wire. The third suffered burns on his hands and feet.

The skunk was unharmed.

And You Thought Pigeons Were a Pain.

The mysterious green blob fell out of the sky and landed near a school in Ripley, Tennessee. No one could figure out what the 25-pound hunk of stuff might be, so the sheriff was called. The blob was put into deep freeze and a sample was sent off to a laboratory at the University of Tennessee for an expert analysis.

In due course, word came back. The green goo had come from the chemical toilet of a commercial airliner. When the toilet's valves are not functioning properly, liquid seeps out and freezes. Growing like an icicle, it finally breaks off and falls.

The Federal Aviation Administration keeps statistics on how many of these have rained down, and so far, the worst year was 1974, when 14 were recorded.

"It's not supposed to happen," said an FAA spokesman, "but it does. We've had them crash into people's kitchens."

Combat Zone.

According to a report issued by the Gun Control Coalition, children in some neighborhoods of New York City have a one percent chance of being shot to death, a greater probability than the average American GI faced during World War II.

Wonderful Golden Rule Days.

Young children are dying by their own hand at an increasing rate, the World Health Organization reports. Prepuberty suicide in the 5-to-14 age group has skyrocketed, says the United Nations organization, with Swedish youngsters leading the way. In Sweden, 13.5 out of every 100,000 5-to-14-year-olds committed suicide in 1976, compared to 0.5 per 100,000 in 1971.

During the 1960s, the organization points out, it was the 15-to-24-year-old group that experienced a sharp rise in self-inflicted death.

A spokesman for the WHO attributes the current trend to an increase in school pressure.

Watch Out.

If you're being interviewed for a job and you're offered a cigarette, you're faced with two possibilities, according to a recent study of corporate hiring procedure. One, the interviewer genuinely likes to smoke and is asking you to share a pleasure. Two, the interviewer hates smoking and your first puff will disqualify you for the job.

The odds, according to the survey: 28 percent of male nonsmokers and 74 percent of female nonsmokers won't consider a smoker for a job.

New Danger.

The American Medical Association warns that seemingly innocent umbrellas are being used with increasing frequency as weapons. The particular problem is that the sharp tip of an umbrella may produce a penetrating head wound that the victim may consider superficial, but which may turn out to be lethal. Anyone stabbed with an umbrella tip should immediately get X rays and brain tests to determine if brain damage has occurred.

One More Thing to Worry About.

A Minnesota man has suffered for five years from nearly continuous farting. After exhaustive medical tests and treatment, ranging from antibiotics and endoscopy to special diets, he has still found no relief. His chronic flatulence causes him to break wind 150 times a day and more. His only relief, in fact, is not to eat.

13
1984

Relax, folks. You can stop worrying about the omnipotent, omni-present government that's due to take over in 1984. The news is, it's already here, and its manipulations are just as absurd—and scary—as George Orwell predicted they'd be.

Silence Is Golden.

In 1979, Leslie C. Dirks received a National Security Medal from President Carter at the White House for "his outstanding contribution in creating and directing a major intelligence program of great national importance."

Mr. Dirks is the CIA's deputy director for science and technology. No reporters or photographers were allowed at the ceremony, and the White House press office told reporters that they didn't have the faintest clue as to what Mr. Dirks had done to get the medal. The information was classified.

Don't Write Things Down.

The Tennessee state senate voted 18 to 14 in favor of removing Tennessee criminal court judge Thomas Galbreath from office, four votes fewer than the two-thirds vote needed to oust him. Galbreath had been charged with misconduct, neglect of duty, and moral turpitude. The reason? In a letter to *Hustler* magazine, written on official stationery, he made an explicit reference to oral sex.

The Majesty of the Law.

George Whitmore, falsely imprisoned for the murders of Jane Wylie and Emily Hofert after police beat him into confessing a crime he did not commit, has been denied the right to sue New York State for damages, because the statute of limitations ran out before he began his suit. Whitmore was in prison for four years before the state's error was discovered and he was released. The statute of limitations is three years.

Law and Order in the City of Brotherly Love.

From 1970 through 1978, Philadelphia police killed 299 people illegally, according to a survey by the Public Interest Law Center, a nonprofit group founded by the Philadelphia Bar Association to help those whose civil rights have been violated. This number, the survey noted, represented more than half of the total of 469 police shootings in this period.

The shootings were clearly illegal, said the center, because none of the victims had been committing a "forcible felony" or had been threatening a police officer's life when they were shot. Ninety-nine were not doing anything criminal; 99 others were later charged with non-violent felonies or misdemeanors.

The survey was released shortly after Philadelphia's mayor, Frank L. Rizzo, testified before the United States Civil Rights Commission and denied that any pattern of police brutality existed in the city. Rizzo was Philadelphia's police commissioner until 1971, when he became mayor.

Suicide.

State police investigating the death of John Paisley, former deputy director of the CIA's Office of Strategic Research, have decided that he committed suicide.

Mr. Paisley's body was found in Chesapeake Bay bound with weights and a bullet hole in the left side of his head.

Police have not explained how a right-handed man could shoot himself in the left side of his head and then tie himself up and jump into the bay.

Keep Up the Good Work.

While the American government spends billions trying to stop smugglers from flying planeloads of marijuana, cocaine, and other illegal drugs into the United States, the Pentagon and the U.S. Customs Service think nothing of selling surplus DC-3s to these same smugglers.

With its ample cargo space, the World War II-vintage DC-3 shapes up as a perfect plane for smuggling —and it can be bought cheap, either directly from the Pentagon or at auctions conducted by government agencies, including the Customs Service. At auction, a DC-3 can be had for as little as $20,000, compared to the $100,000 smugglers would have to pay for a smaller, commercial twin-engined plane. Planes sold at Customs Service auctions are often confiscated from drug smugglers, and end up in other smugglers' hands at the auction.

Peter Bensinger, administrator of the Drug Enforcement Administration, admits it's "frustrating" to find that the same airplane has been used by different smugglers. But he doesn't think the government will change the way it handles surplus plane sales. "Anyway," he noted, "the government can use the money it gets from the plane sales."

Keep Them Moving.

The government of South Africa insists it is devoted to the best interests of its black citizens. But consider this: A bill has been introduced in the Parliament of South Africa that would make it a crime for any black in the country to be unemployed. The country already has a law that limits the number of blacks any business can employ. Since it was passed in 1968, 50,000 blacks have lost their jobs, and every day 1,000 more blacks are losing theirs. As a result, an estimated 30 percent of the country's black males are currently unemployed.

The new law would permit the government to deport any unemployed black to a work colony in a nonwhite area for up to two years, and deprive him of his right to reenter urban areas, where the jobs are. This law is called the " Idle Bantu Bill," but obviously it's Catch-22.

Communicate by ESP Only.

Cal Rowley, known as the "one-man vice squad" of the Seattle Police Department, is determined to bolster his record of having more prostitution arrests than any other Seattle police officer.

Rowley's latest weapon in the war against vice is a lip reader who accompanies Rowley as he tries to round up prostitutes. Under the city's antiprostitution law, a police officer must observe prostitutes soliciting in a public place, and from a distance an officer can't know exactly what the women are saying. Hence the lip reader.

Captain Dale Douglass, head of the vice squad, is all for the new gimmick: "If the judge will buy it," Captain Douglass said, "it will open up a whole new area for us."

Why We Need Nuclear Weapons.

China may be trying to modernize its economy, but it seems to be quite happy to have old-fashioned infantrymen. In the 1979 Chinese attack on Vietnam, these infantrymen used tactics reminiscent of the "human wave" techniques the Chinese favored when they fought against the United States in the Korean War, charging into battle to the sound of bugles, hurling themselves against the enemy with no thought of protecting their own lives, sometimes deliberately stepping on Vietnamese mines to clear the way for their comrades to advance.

The Chinese press agency Hsinhua reported, for example, that one deputy company commander grabbed a rocket launcher from one of his wounded men and charged up a hill as the bugle sounded, wiping out seven Vietnamese soldiers with a submachine gun when he reached their trench.

Another Chinese soldier, said Hsinhua, volunteered to blow up a Vietnamese machine gun in a bunker. When he reached it and found that there was no way he could possibly attach the charge to the outside of the bunker, he lit the explosive's fuse with his right hand as he held it in his left, and then, waiting for the charge to explode, waved to his comrades to move forward.

Freedom.

According to a transcript of the trial of a Peking underground newspaper editor, the prosecutor explained that the principles of the Chinese constitution provide that "The citizen has only the freedom to support these principles and not the freedom to oppose them." When the transcript was mimeographed and sold to the public by another underground paper, its staff was immediately arrested.

And Your Name Goes on the List of People Who Bought This Book.

For $5, you can obtain a 750-page book issued by the General Accounting Office that lists all the people the federal government has denoted as being of special interest to it. There are 6,600 separate lists in the book, each list compiled by a different government department or agency. The longest listing originated in the Department of Defense, and consists of 169 pages of the names of those who show "a constant interest in arms-related subjects."

Reading Is a Crime.

Frank Giese, a former professor at Portland State University in Oregon was brought to trial charged with participating in the bombing of a Portland military recruitment center in 1973.

During the trial, the prosecution submitted as evidence a book entitled *From the Movement Toward Revolution*, a documentary history of the "New Left." Giese's fingerprints, the prosecution pointed out, appeared on many pages of the book in which violent action was advocated.

The jury convicted Giese of conspiracy and, on appeal, two federal judges on the San Francisco Appeals Court ruled that indeed the book was relevant evidence and that the conspiracy conviction should stand.

The dissenting judge, Shirley Hufstedler, said: "Even during the evil thralldom of McCarthyism, we did not embrace the concept of guilt by book association."

Democracy.

In repeated experiments, most Americans shown the Bill of Rights or polled about its guarantees considered it subversive. In the latest study in Maine, where a high school teacher had his 11th-grade class circulate a petition to repeal these amendments to the Constitution, an average of 71 percent offered their signatures.

Ill Health.

In 1979, Afghanistan's state radio announced that President Noor Mohammad Taraki had resigned "for reasons of ill health." Not mentioned: 12 bullet holes in his body.

Don't Ask Questions.

Don't call the Internal Revenue Service if you want accurate information on how to fill out your tax return. That, at least, is the advice of the General Accounting Office, the agency that keeps track of how other federal agencies operate.

For a number of years, GAO personnel, pretending to be ordinary taxpayers, have been calling IRS information officers across the country to ask the kind of questions taxpayers might ask, and they've been receiving some wrong answers from the supposedly in-the-know income tax experts.

But the IRS is improving its performance. In 1977, the GAO got a wrong answer, on the average, for every fourth question it asked. In 1978, the IRS did better, answering an average of 9 out of 10 questions correctly.

Of course, even one wrong answer is too many, particularly since the IRS insists that if you fill out your return incorrectly on the basis of an answer you got from them, it's tough luck, Charlie. You're still liable for interest and penalties for the mistake you —that is, the IRS—made.

Meet Thomas Jefferson, Communist Hippie Raver.

Miami *Herald* reporter Colin Dangaard approached 50 people with a typed copy of the Declaration of Independence and asked each of them to sign it. Only one person would do so. Many of the others reviled him for presenting an un-American document. Two called it "Commie junk." Another wai.ted to tell the FBI "about this sort of rubbish." Others called the document's author "a hippie," "a raver," "a red-neck revolutionist," and "a person of Communism, someone against our country."

Oubliette.

Andreas Mihawecz was arrested in the small town of Hochst, Austria, for questioning in connection with an automobile accident, and thrown into a cell in the town's small jail.

His jailers forgot completely about their prisoner. Mihawecz shouted frantically for help—to no avail—when he realized that no guard was coming to feed him. To relieve the pain of hunger, he tried to eat his leather jacket and he drank his own urine.

Eighteen days later, Mihawecz was found by accident. He was near death, and though doctors said he would probably survive, they also predicted he would suffer from kidney disease as a result of his starvation bout.

Austria's minister of the interior announced that he was ordering an investigation to discover how the incident could have occurred.

Only Pinkos and Fellow Travelers Complain.

Mrs. Martha Laird lived on a Nevada ranch 80 miles north of the Nevada test site at which above-ground testing took place from 1951 to 1963. Testifying before a joint congressional committee hearing investigating the connection of atomic tests to the increase of cancer-related deaths in Nevada and southern Utah, Mrs. Laird said that the government never told her and her family anything about the possible effects of radiation.

"At no time," she said, "did the Atomic Energy Commission come and test our water and food. All this time we were feeding our children and families poison from these bombs. We were forgotten guinea pigs. At least real guinea pigs are checked."

Mrs. Laird's son and husband both got leukemia after the tests, and her son died.

The Atomic Energy Commission carried out 87 above-ground atomic tests in the 1950s, which could have affected 170,000 people in a 300-mile radius of the test site. Since the tests, more than 500 cancer victims have sued the Department of Energy for millions of dollars, claiming that the cancer deaths resulted from government negligence in not warning of radioactive danger.

Mrs. Laird told the committee that she had written to the government a number of times about her family's illness, but she had never received a satisfactory reply. In one letter, the government told her that her complaints were "communistically-inspired."

14
Awards
&
Citations

Too often, talent, skill, perseverance, industry, integrity, and all those other qualities vital to success in our complicated society go unrecognized in the hurly-burly of daily life. To remedy this sad oversight, we present our monitor of awards and citations that never make the headlines—but should.

The Scientific Heroism Cup.

After a two-month battle that cost $1,000 a day, government workers have put out a fire in huge deposits of ancient Shasta sloth dung in a remote Grand Canyon cave. Fire-fighting efforts were hampered by scientists who wanted the 80,000-year-old-droppings left as undisturbed as possible.

"We had to go in there and spot-wet it and try to smother it with asbestos blankets and CO_2 gas," said Forestry Service technician Dave Stiegelmeyer. "At one point the roof caved in and we had to shore it up with timbers.

"It was like being in a cave full of burning shit. The temperature was 200–250° Fahrenheit and visibility was zero. The smoke was too thick for our lights to penetrate it. We had to feel our way around the cave in complete darkness and locate the burning parts by their heat. It was terrifying.

"Normally, we would have just sealed the cave and let it burn itself out."

Much of the expense was for helicopters at $260 an hour, but the terrain was so rough that workers had to hike more than a mile and a half in 120° F. summer heat carrying 60-pound packs and wearing heat-retarding armor. Stiegelmeyer was paid $5 an hour plus overtime.

Forestry Service officials were unclear as to the scientific value of the sloth dung. Requests for further information directly from the scientists have received no response so far.

The Order of Sanity.

"Have a nice day" has been singled out for special dishonor by the Unicorn Hunters, a group of word-people at Lake Superior State College, in Michigan, who point out that telephone operators say this even when dealing with customers calling funeral homes.

The Kafka Cross.

Dennis Soyster, a credit manager for a Maryland carpet company, was told that he was dying. Doctors did an exploratory operation and told him his stomach problem was the result of a rare, but always terminal, intestinal disease.

Soyster decided that, if he was going, he would go in style, and he stole $29,000 from the carpet company to finance one last wild fling of high living. After he had spent the $29,000 on his spree, the doctors changed their minds. In reality, they said, his problem was that he was allergic to the surgical gloves worn by the medics who'd operated on him.

Charged with embezzlement, Soyster was given a suspended sentence and ordered to repay the money in installments of $5,000 a year.

Soyster now has a new job: He's a credit manager for a loan company.

Keeping Christmas Holy Banner.

A toilet seat that plays the Ohio University fight song and a pornographic ashtray given to a 60-year-old couple were among the entries received in the "Worst of Christmas" contest sponsored by the Reverend Bob Kochitsky of Jackson, Mississippi, who organized the awards to fight the commercialization of Christmas.

No Wonder Johnny Can't Read Ribbon.

Southeast Missouri State University offers a summer school course in UFOs. Upon payment of the $50 course fee, students receive a "scientific kit" to help spot UFOs, and a week's instruction from UFO authority Harley Rutledge. The course is worth two credits at the university.

King Solomon's Star.

Mrs. Lynn Blake of New York City sued her landlord for $2 million in damages, accusing the landlord of harassment for attempting to evict her from her apartment, and accusing the landlord's agent of sexual assault.

Acting as her own lawyer, Mrs. Blake presented her case in October, 1979, to a New York City judge and a six-person jury. She charged that the landlord had harassed her for 10 years by not collecting garbage, failing to control rodents in the building, and failing to provide adequate heat and hot water.

The jury awarded Mrs. Blake the $2 million in damages. Two months later, however, the judge reversed the jury's finding. He ruled that the pattern of harassment was not proved, and that the charge of sexual assault was "very innocuous." In view of this, the judge said, Mrs. Blake was entitled not to the $2 million in damages, but to six cents.

Mrs. Blake has filed a new suit in New York State Supreme Court, again asking for $2 million in damages.

The Devotion to Commerce Certificate.

Five brokers, four clerks, and three other financial wizards at the Chicago Board of Options Exchange, where millions of dollars change hands each day, traded in cocaine at the same time they were trading in options to buy securities—until they were arrested by agents of the United States Drug Enforcement Administration.

For those who wondered if the exchange's traders were *using* the coke, exchange board President William M. Smith was reassuring, telling investors that their money was in no greater jeopardy than usual.

Drinker of the Year.

Nineteen-year-old Teryl Barth of Wind Lake, Wisconsin, put on a drinking show for 50 customers in a local bar. He ordered the bartender to serve him five drinks at a time, the round to consist of a shot of 150-proof rum, 100-proof Yukon Jack, 90-proof Jack Daniels, 100-proof Southern Comfort, and 80-proof brandy. Barth downed five shots one after another, then ordered the next round.

On his tenth round, after four hours of drinking, during which he consumed 46 shots, Barth slumped down, out cold. He remained unconscious and died some time later.

Peace Nomination.

Pet lovers who can't get over how divine their pets are can now do something about the feeling. The Universal Pet Church will issue an ornate Certificate of Ordination installing dog, cat, turtle, gerbil, whatever, as a Minister of God in the Universal Pet Church. The church "proudly recognizes the sacred qualities of God's most trusted and noble creatures," and its certificates feature the slogan "Universal Peace Through Pets." (The cost, $2.50 by mail, P.O. Box 12514, Denver, Colorado 80212.)

Worst Contest.

The International Cherry Pit Spitting Contest has been held annually for the past six years in the southwest Michigan community of Eau Claire. The 1978 winner, William A. Mobley (called "Pits"), outdistanced all other entrants by propelling a pit 49 feet, 2 inches. Contestants for the contest practice for weeks before the event, spitting as many as 100 pits a day. The winner receives a rental cherry tree from a local orchard. The runner-up gets a bucket of pits to practice with.

Best Music Critic.

John McNutt, an Iowa City, Iowa, hog raiser, probably knows more about pigs' taste in music than anyone.

For the past couple of years, McNutt has been playing recorded music in his hog pens, and these are his findings: Pigs are most tranquil and gain weight the fastest when they listen to classical music. Rock 'n' roll, on the other hand, gets the pigs upset. And when opera is played, they start climbing the walls.

Lawyer of the Year.

On trial for purse-snatching in Tulsa, Oklahoma, a nonlegal type named Marshall Cummings decided to serve as his own counsel. Things went well until he asked the woman whose purse he was accused of grabbing the following question: "Did you get a good look at my face when I took your purse?"

Cummings is now serving a 10-year sentence in the Oklahoma State Penitentiary.

How to Run a Government Commendation.

It now costs the Royal Canadian Mint two cents to make a penny and six cents to make a nickel.

The Ride-Him-out-of-Texas-on-a-Rail Medal.

This one goes to Houston Police Chief Harry Caldwell, whose men are fit to be barbecued because the chief has refused to permit them to wear cowboy boots on duty.

Jesse James Memorial.

For the first time in California history, someone's been convicted of bee rustling. The culprit is David Allred, 23, who was sentenced in Stockton to three years for stealing $10,000 worth of beehives.

Allred told the judge he hoped to be remembered as "the Jesse James of the bee industry."

The Citation for Off-Beat Rural Beautification.

To a bored but energetic weatherman in Her Majesty's Canadian Service. Serving a two-year tour in a desolate area of northern Canada, he made use of an abandoned Royal Air Force bulldozer and some surveying equipment to rearrange millions of tons of boulders, earth and ice. When he had finished, four colossal letters were spread out over the countryside. They spelled the familiar English obscenity for sexual intercourse—"F-U-C-K." The giant word is still there, somewhat north of Hudson Bay. It's clearly visible from planes on intercontinental routes flying as high as 27,000 feet, but somehow commercial pilots never point it out to their passengers.

For Public Service.

Millionaire United States Senator Herman Talmadge, explaining how he managed to write just two checks, (they totaled $600) for cash from 1970 to 1976: "Wherever I go, people entertain me, lodge me, give me small amounts of money. My out-of-pocket expenses come from donations friends give me, five dollars, a ten-dollar bill, sometimes fifteen or twenty dollars. They come up and say they know I have a lot of expenses back in Washington and they want to help me."

Isn't This Stupid Prize.

Ten University of Maine students executed what they called a three-hour "horizontal climb"—in other words, a crawl—along a street between two campus buildings. Why did these adventurers decide to "climb" the flat street? Said one, "Simply because it's there."

Crime-of-the-Month-Club

Crime and books go together so well. Someone ought to do a doctoral thesis on the number of books written as a result of Watergate. What will the bookstores have next? What else but the Crime-of-the-Month Club, which is what could happen if the Book-of-the-Month Club were raped by the Mafia. The Club doesn't just buy books about crimes, it buys the crimes themselves wholesale and sells them retail. The Main Selection is handled like Watergate. There are national political power struggles about the release of the materials. *The New York Times* runs banner headlines. The careers of investigative reporters are made. Massive televised show trials are sponsored by consortiums of advertisers. But you get the picture. Onward to smug self-congratulation about the role of the press in participatory democracy.

Main Selection: Hungry Man.

Naomi Anderson of Morganton, North Carolina, is determined to see justice done. She's sworn out a warrant against 18-year-old Keith Sturling, charging him with injury to personal property.

The personal property in question is her pet boa constrictor. It was resting peacefully in the back seat of her car when Sturling came along, and according to Ms. Anderson, bit off a half inch of the snake's tail.

How did this get to be the winner? When was the last time you read a man-bites-snake story?

P.S. Sturling was fined $100.

1st Alternate: Hitler Made Me Do It.

In the West German town of Klingenberg, a 23-year-old epileptic student named Annaliese Muhe refused to eat, rejected medical attention, and ultimately wasted away to 70 pounds before she died.

Her parents and two Roman Catholic priests were convicted of negligent homicide in her death. By their own admission, the priests and parents had not called in a doctor because the girl had "placed her fate in the hand of God in order to free herself from the demons who possessed her." Instead, they tried to exorcise these demons.

The priests testified that the girl had, in fact, been possessed by evil spirits. She said that she wanted to die to atone for the sins of others, particularly the sins of German youth.

The priests forced two of the demons to identify themselves as "Hitler" and "Nero." One priest made Hitler recite the Hail Mary prayer in an exorcism rite to drive out this devil. The rite failed, as did all others, and the demons continued to possess the girl until she died.

2nd Alternate: Mrs. Detra Made Me Do It.

A Kingsburg, California, woman, who is accused of conspiring to murder her husband, has come with a creative defense.

The attorney for 52-year-old Edith Robinson said his client should not be found guilty of hiring a man to kill her husband, because she was under the influence of the psychic/astrologer, Madame Rosalie Detra.

The attorney said Madame Detra had successfully predicted that the twin brother of Mrs. Robinson's husband would die in a construction accident. Then he said Madame Detra told Mrs. Robinson her husband would also die. Madame Detra made these predictions from trances which she prepared for by standing in front of a cross, reading from the Bible, and praying to the president of the United States.

After the prediction, the attorney said, Mrs. Robinson was "in torment," thinking her husband would die at any time. "She wanted it over with," he added, and tried to hasten the death by burning a lock of her husband's hair, some of his socks, and his photograph.

When that didn't work, she got the idea of hiring someone to kill her husband. Shortly thereafter, her daughter introduced her to a man who said he'd do it for $10,000. He turned out to be an undercover police officer.

Mrs. Robinson has pleaded not guilty by reason of insanity.

3rd Alternate: How Bad Is British Plumbing?

M rs. Eileen Finlay, a British housewife whose husband committed suicide, hid his body in the cupboard for 20 months because she feared the police would accuse her of killing him. The body was found by a janitor after Mrs. Finlay finally moved it to a refuse area in her building.

After her husband's death, Mrs. Finlay allowed a new boyfriend to move into her apartment. He was unaware of the corpse in the cupboard. On numerous occasions, however, he complained of an awful smell in the apartment.

Mrs. Finlay told him it came from clogged drains.

Collegian of the Year.

Does college teach youth ingenuity? On the basis of the following story, the answer has to be: Sometimes.

At Stanford University, recently, a professor giving a final exam in chemistry warned his class of more than 400 students that he would positively not accept test papers—written in the traditional blue book—that were handed in after he had called "time."

Ten minutes after the test was over, the blue books resting in a large loose pile on the desk, one student tried to turn his in. The professor refused to accept it. The student pleaded, the professor was adamant.

The student finally had a thought. "Do you know my name?" he asked the professor. The professor owned up to his ignorance.

The student smiled. Quickly and deftly, he slipped his book into the middle of the pile and walked out of the classroom.

Best Graffiti.

"Illiterate? Write for free brochure."

"If you have taken a shit, bring it back immediately, no questions asked."

15
Endings

"What is the answer?" Gertrude Stein was asked as she lay dying. "What is the question?" Gertrude Stein replied. In the no man's land called life that is bounded by these two inquiries, what could be more absurd than the fact that no one has yet been able to produce a definitive answer to either.

Slow Death.

Marc Quinquandon, 27, of Nancy, France, died in a hospital after swallowing six dozen snails in less than three minutes at a dance hall. The 368-pound truck driver had been declared winner of the "Olympic Games of Absurdities" in nearby Thiaucourt earlier in the year after eating 144 snails in 11½ minutes.

Fearless Ingenuity.

Philip Bachman, an American inventor, has come up with his own special solution to a worldwide problem: Diminishing space for cemeteries. He begins by immersing a corpse in liquid nitrogen, at minus 150° Fahrenheit. This solidifies body tissues, an essential for the next step, which occurs when the body is placed in a hammer mill and smashed into tiny pieces. The pieces are then freeze-dried, which knocks out 96 percent of the body that is water. What's left can then be sealed for burial or put in an urn to be displayed.

Brave New World.

Americans are becoming less fearful of premature death and this could mean that fewer people will be buying life insurance, worries the American Council of Life Insurance, an industry trade association, in a special report.

The council said that by the year 2000 life expectancy will be 90. Euthanasia will be legal. Terminally ill patients will be permitted to "program their own deaths in any way they see fit," and many will choose ample doses of heroin.

Death will be painless if a person so chooses. Most will, and consequently will face death calmly and without fear, they say.

Never Say Die.

When his mother, Gladys Rogers, died at the age of 80, evangelist Daniel Aaron Rogers put her body in a freezer and then began to pray over it. He was convinced that since "Jesus commanded us to preach the Gospel, heal the sick and raise the dead," he would be able to bring his mother back to life.

Rogers and three other evangelists prayed over the freezer for two hours, while their congregations waited in a nearby chapel for the miracle to occur, moaning, crying, and praying in support of their preachers.

After the prayer session, one of the evangelists, J. T. Williams, said: "We have tried everything Jesus told us to do, and we don't know what is wrong. She has not risen from the dead."

Rogers remained confident. "We have not given up," he said. "We fully expect the resurrection to happen."

The day before the prayer session Rogers told reporters: "We expect Momma to be raised. A neighbor of one of my associate evangelists said she had a vision, and she saw Momma open her eyes and get up." Rogers said that he believed the resurrection of his mother would be a signal that Christ is coming and that "the end of this age as we know it, would be near." This would mean that "the wicked will be burned up, by fire...we believe by atomic bomb fire." That wouldn't happen the day after his mother was "raised," Rogers said, but "the time will be near. The righteous, the good people, they will survive. Just the extremely wicked are going to be destroyed."

An Unusual Accident.

Adolf Daxboeck, of Burnaby, British Columbia, was having a contest with his girlfriend to see how far each could "throw" a Ping-Pong ball by blowing it out of their mouths. Daxboeck put a ball in his mouth and then, apparently, tried to take a deep breath to increase his "throwing power." Instead, he swallowed the ball and choked to death when it became lodged in his throat.

If They Were So Great, What Happened to Them?

An advertisement for the German-built Audi automobile that appeared in British publications called the brontosaurus "arguably the worst-designed creature of all time."

Numerous dinosaur lovers, both expert and amateur, became incensed and, in the British tradition of fair play, came to the defense of the extinct animal. The advertisement, they insisted, had clearly maligned the creature. In a typical comment, Dr. Alan Charing of the British Museum noted, "Brontosauruses survived for about 140 million years—rather longer than we shall manage, I suspect—and were miracles of engineering. Everything they did, they did successfully."

Miami Beach Is Nicer.

While the American hostages were being held by Iranian militants in the United States Embassy in Teheran, a newspaper owner in the city of Qum offered an all-expenses paid pilgrimage to Mecca to the person who would murder the Shah. The Iranian government had previously announced that killing the former ruler of the country would be considered a legal act.

Final Sale.

A $6 cardboard coffin is offered by mortician Ken Timlick of Vancouver, British Columbia. For another $3, his wife, Jean, will sew a satinlike lining and pillows. "It's clearly a triumph," says Ken.

Better Shelf Life.

American funeral directors have noticed that corpses do not decompose as quickly as they used to. They attribute this development to the increased use of preservatives in convenience and packaged foods.

No Trespassing.

The police in Rio de Janeiro are very concerned about criminals breaking municipal regulations, and so they recently made the following announcement:

"The new cemetery in São Joao de Meriti has not been officially opened. Therefore, we wish to emphasize that murderers should refrain from dumping the dead bodies of victims on this site, as lately has frequently happened."

Keep on Trucking.

It's tough enough and tragic enough to determine when a human is legally and medically dead. Tougher still, it turns out, for entomologists to figure out exactly when an insect has died. For example: Take out a fly's heart and it will go right on living without missing a buzz. Cut off its head and ultimately it will die, but only because it no longer can eat.

This state of affairs has complicated the lives of entomologists, and, at last, they've adopted a dead-fly rule. To wit: "A fly is considered dead if it doesn't move for twenty-four to forty-eight hours."

This is good, but a word to living flies is in order: Stay out of the laboratory scotch.

The Love of Money Is the Root of All Evil.

James Scott, Duke of Monmouth, about to be executed by a notoriously clumsy headsman, offered the man six guineas to do the job well, plus the promise of more from his servant after the deed was done. This so unnerved the executioner that he totally botched the job, hacking at the condemned man's neck over and over again before severing it.